Little Prisoners

SUNDAY TIMES BESTSELLING AUTHOR

CASEY WATSON

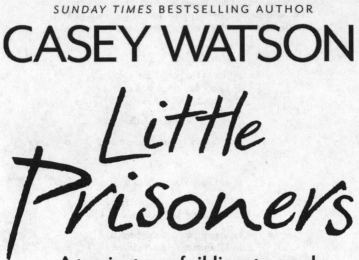

Little
Prisoners

A tragic story of siblings trapped in a world of abuse and suffering

This book is a work of non-fiction based on the author's experiences.
In order to protect privacy, names, identifying characteristics,
dialogue and details have been changed or reconstructed.

HarperElement
An Imprint of HarperCollins*Publishers*
1 London Bridge Street
London SE1 9GF

www.harpercollins.co.uk

First published by HarperElement 2012

1

A catalogue record of this book is
available from the British Library

ISBN 978-0-00-743660-6

Printed and bound in the United States of
America by RR Donnelley

Find out more about HarperCollins and the environment at
www.harpercollins.co.uk/green

To my wonderful and supportive family

Acknowledgements

I would like to thank all of the team at HarperCollins, the lovely Andrew Lownie, and my friend and mentor, Lynne.

Chapter 1

My husband, Mike, always bagged the window seat on planes, so I had to lean across him to watch ours land. He ruffled my hair.

'Hey, look at you, eager beaver!' he said. 'Can't wait to get home again, can you?'

We were returning from a glorious week in Corfu. Just the two of us. A rare break, and one we really needed. We'd just said goodbye to our most recent foster child, Sophia, and the impromptu holiday had been a real tonic. Sophia's had been a two-week emergency stay that had stretched to almost a year. It had also been a pretty bumpy ride.

I snuggled up as far as my seat belt would let me, anxious to reassure him that that wasn't the case. Well, not quite. 'Oh, love,' I said. 'It's been a *fantastic* holiday, *really*. But you know what I'm like. I'm missing the kids now. Especially baby Levi.'

1

Levi was our little grandson and one of the joys in our lives. 'I know,' Mike said, squeezing over so I could see out. 'Me too, if I'm honest. But we'll be home in next to no time … ah, here we go. Let's see how he lands it.'

We both watched as the plane seemed to float towards the runway. No bumps today. The pilot touched down perfectly.

Looking after Sophia, who was now 13, and in temporary residential care, while they tackled her mental health problems, had been an experience we wouldn't forget in a hurry. The outlook was positive, and we were still seeing her regularly, but what we'd been through when she was with us had taken its toll. Not just on the poor child but on us as a family, and now we were safely back on terra firma I realised just how much I needed to see my own children. Riley, my eldest, and mother to my gorgeous Levi, had given us the news, just the evening before we'd left, that she was now pregnant with our second grandchild. We'd been so thrilled, and now I was itching to get back to her and give her another hug.

I also couldn't wait to see Kieron, our son, who I knew wouldn't relax till he had us safely home again. He has Asperger's syndrome and one of its features is that changes in routine made him anxious. Though he'd been away himself for a few days' holiday with his girlfriend Lauren and her family, I knew it wouldn't stop him fretting about whether we were okay.

And now we'd touched down, I couldn't wait to actually get home and see them, so getting away from Manchester

Airport couldn't happen soon enough. I hate airports, especially in the middle of the day, when they're at their busiest, and today wasn't going to be an exception. We were herded along blindly down endless white corridors, then, due to all the extra security procedures, stood in one interminable queue after another. I sometimes wondered if we wouldn't be better off going by boat. Finally, we emerged into the baggage reclaim area, but typically, there was no baggage yet in sight.

Sod this, I thought. I hadn't had a cigarette in ages. 'Mike,' I said, making a familiar gesture. 'D'you mind waiting for the cases, love, and I'll see you outside?'

He smiled indulgently, bless him. 'Go on, then,' he said. Which was kind of him – as a non-smoker, I knew how much he wished I'd give up. Which I would, very soon. But not today. Giving him a quick peck, I headed off towards the arrivals hall and outside, rummaging in my handbag for my cigarettes as I went.

As I did so, I also pulled out my mobile. Time to switch it back on and catch up with everyone. I was particularly keen to speak to Riley, of course, just to check all was well with the new pregnancy. Plus I knew she might be anxious to speak to me too. We were close, and she knew just how much looking after Sophia had taken out of me. I knew she'd would want to catch up.

My thoughts were confirmed within seconds of turning my phone on. A series of bleeps, as text after text began appearing – though the texts, I could see, were all from voicemail. Hmm, I thought. Someone's keen to welcome me back. The much-needed cigarette shelved for the moment, I dialled voicemail, put my ear to the phone and listened.

It hadn't been Riley, but they were all from the same person. John Fulshaw, the link worker at the fostering agency Mike and I worked for. They'd all been made today, and were all pretty much identical. *'Casey, can you please call me as soon as you get this?'*

I was immediately alert. This could only mean one thing. That he must have another child in mind for us.

Mike appeared then, dragging both our cases behind him. They'd obviously not taken as long as we'd expected. I waved my mobile at him. 'Hey, guess what?' I said to him, my grin widening at the prospect. 'John's been on the phone, leaving messages!'

'Bloody hell, Case!' he said. 'We've only just touched down! What messages? What does he want?'

I shook my head. 'I don't know yet. But I'm hoping it's another kid.'

Mike rolled his eyes at me. 'Already?' Then he grinned. 'Go on, then. Ring him. Might as well do it now.'

My excitement mounting, I dialled the now familiar number. Over the past couple of years, we'd grown very close to John. These days he was more of a friend than a boss, and I felt I was becoming used to all his little ways. He was a born worrier and he sounded worried now.

'Oh, thank God, Casey!' he said. 'I was beginning to think I had my dates wrong. You are back in the UK now, are you? You're not still on hols?'

'No, we're here,' I said. 'What's up? You sounded slightly panicked on voicemail.'

'"Slightly" is putting it mildly,' he answered. 'We've been landed with a real emergency situation, and, to be frank, I have nowhere else to turn.'

'Go on,' I said, even more intrigued now. I couldn't help it. For all the lows of my job, this bit was one of the highs. This part when you had no idea what was just around the corner. What the child would be like, what their problems might be, what grim circumstances they'd come from and why.

I heard him take a breath. 'Look, I hate to put this on you, Casey. And you can say no if you want, you know that, don't you? But well, it's a sibling placement. Two children …'

'Two kids. Oh, my!'

'Yes,' he confirmed. 'Young ones. Older boy, younger girl. And it's a desperate situation – they have to be moved as soon as possible. They've both been grossly neglected and are – or so I'm told – in a terrible state. And that's both mentally and physically.'

'Physically? Have they been hurt?'

'No, it's nothing like that. Well, as far as we know, it isn't. More neglect. Serious neglect. They've been living a bit like animals. It'll be a challenge, Casey, I'm not going to lie to you. They have some issues. Their behaviour will need managing. The only thing I *can* say is that it's going to be an extremely short placement. Just interim. Two weeks, three at the most.'

'Well,' I said, gesturing to Mike, who was watching intently. 'You know what I'm like – always up for a new challenge. And the two of them … what ages?'

'Erm, six and nine, I think. Or thereabouts.'

Little ones, then. In comparison with my last child, for sure. 'Look,' I said. 'I'm obviously going to have to run this by Mike first.' Mike's eyebrows rose. 'Make sure he's happy with it, okay? Can I call you back?"

''Course you can.'

I chose my words carefully as I relayed all this to Mike. I wasn't sure if I was hoping he'd say no to it or not. On the one hand, it was an exciting new challenge – albeit a brief one. But two badly neglected young children. That was completely new territory. I was used to having one difficult-to-place child at a time. Two of them together, and so young – that was something to think about. It had always been teenagers who were my natural forte. Challenging teenagers, yes. But not little ones!

There was also the question of it being short term again, though this wasn't entirely unexpected. It *was* a bit annoying – after all, Mike and I had trained as specialist carers, employed to work to an innovative behaviour modification model – but along with others like us, we'd already been warned that due to government cutbacks we had to be flexible, and that we might be required to undertake *any* kind of fostering, in order to meet the council's needs. I supposed it was sensible – better to be utilised than sit around waiting for a child who met our model's criteria. But even so, it felt a shame not to be able to do what we'd trained for – we'd done it with our first placement, Justin, and had really seen the benefits. But, hey ho. Such was life in the public sector. And the words 'badly neglected' triggered something maternal inside me. Poor mites. What grim story would they have to tell?

Mike was looking at me, considering, as he took in what I'd told him. 'Two little ones,' he said. 'And one of them only six? That's going to take it out of you, love. You have thought of that, have you?'

Which, of course, sent me straight into overdrive. Finally lighting my cigarette, I fell into step with him as we made our way to the long-stay car park. Stuff and nonsense, I told him. I was in my early forties, not my dotage! Plus I'd already been reminded how tiring little ones could be. Now we had Levi in our lives, it had all come right back. And I pooh-poohed his comment that Levi didn't actually *live* with us. I was fired up now. *Of course* we'd be able to manage, I told him. How difficult could they be? Anyway, I pointed out, it was the summer holidays, wasn't it? So no school stress to fret about. And I could take them out, keep them occupied. To the park. To the swimming pool, to the cinema and so on. And Riley would help. Little Levi would love it. And it wouldn't be for long, I reminded him.

But his face, when I was done, still had doubt etched across it. 'Look love,' he said. 'It's you I'm thinking of here. I'll be at work. It's you that'll have to deal with them.' We'd reached the car park by now and he turned as we passed the barrier. 'But if you think you can do it, go on, call John back. Say yes. I have a feeling you're not going to take no for an answer, anyway, so we might as well put him out of his misery.'

I leaned across and kissed him. 'We can do it, love. "We" being the operative word here ...'

'Hey,' he said. 'I can still change my mind, you know!'

But he didn't. He wouldn't. He knew what I was like. I gleefully grabbed my mobile and began dialling.

Twenty-four hours later, and the house was a hive of activity. I'd been thrilled by the children's response to the news; after Sophia, whose problems had caused the whole family a lot of heartache, I had expected them to be a lot more reticent. Instead, Kieron was already enthusing about how he and Lauren could take them bowling, and even Riley, though more reserved, and also quick to point out how much hard work young kids were – just like her father! – was happy to pitch in.

We had a four-bed house, one bedroom housing Mike and I, and one housing Kieron, and the third bedroom was currently a confection of pink butterflies and fairy princesses, the way we'd decorated when Sophia had come to live with us. Given the little ones wouldn't be with us for long, it made sense not to go overboard changing things. The pink room would happily house the little girl who was coming, and her brother could go in the fourth bedroom, the spare room, which was currently home to Kieron and his college friend's DJing equipment – all the mixers, amps and decks essential to the making of new tracks. It really just needed a good clear-out and clean up, and all the contents transferring to the garden shed.

We'd had some more info by now, from an extremely grateful John, who, had he been able to crawl along the phone line and hug me, would, I could tell, have probably done so. As it was, he just had to content himself with thanking me profusely and letting me know we'd have everyone's full support. The children now had names at least; the nine-year-old boy was called Ashton, and his six-year-old sister was Olivia.

I'd get more in the afternoon, he said, when the social worker called me, but in the meantime he wanted to let me know that a new bed was already on its way. Happily, Mike, who was a warehouse manager and very busy with his own job, had taken two days off to get the rooms straight, so I could at least be sure the children would both have somewhere nice and welcoming to sleep.

By lunchtime, I was happy that we were getting things organised, so, leaving Mike and Kieron painting – they'd found a big tin of blue emulsion, left over from when we'd decorated for our first foster child, Justin – Riley and I made a trip into town for some bits. I knew it wasn't really necessary, but the word 'neglect' kept jumping out at me, so even if they would be with us only a short while I was determined these poor little ones would find the experience a positive one. It would take no time at all to grab some bits from all the local charity shops: books to read, toys and jigsaws, soft toys and dolls – just some kiddie paraphernalia to help make them feel at home.

Riley and I were just staggering back in through the front door with our haul when the phone rang. As promised, it was the children's social worker.

'I'm Anna,' she told me. She sounded young and very professional. 'And I can't tell you how grateful we are that you've agreed to help us out. John's told us so much about you and Mike, and we really don't know what we'd have done without you. And I have to tell you ...' I mentally braced, because the tone of her voice had now changed markedly, '... that the situation's become somewhat more urgent.'

I wasn't sure what she meant. In the world in which we worked we were used to pretty much everything being urgent. Well, if *they* needed something, anyway – it didn't necessarily work in reverse. 'More urgent?'

'In that we've had to give the parents notice. That we're going to be removing the children in the morning ...'

'The morning? You mean tomorrow morning?'

'I'm afraid so,' she answered. 'We would have moved them today, but of course it was only fair to give you notice ...'

'But what about the pre-placement meeting? We know absolutely nothing about them.'

I should have expected this, I thought ruefully as I waited for her answer. In theory, before a child is placed with a foster family, there is a defined process – a formal meeting, in which all concerned parties are present, so that social services can give the new carers some background and so that a plan of action for the child

Little Prisoners

or children's future can be put in place. But in practice … Hmm, I thought, we'd been here before, hadn't we?

'I'm so sorry,' she said, 'to land the two of you in it like this. We will, of course, arrange an urgent meeting with you, once you have the children, then we can tell you both everything we know.'

I could almost hear her holding her breath, waiting for me to argue. But I'd committed, and these kids needed a temporary home, *now*.

'Okay,' I said.

'Oh, thank you *so*, *so* much,' she answered. Rather worryingly.

After a fitful night mostly spent making mental lists, the following morning found me sitting in my garden, drinking in its glorious summer scents. It was looking – and smelling – particularly gorgeous, as Kieron had cut the grass for me, and Lauren had done some weeding. It would be the perfect place, I thought, for these poor, sad little children, to run around and let off some steam.

I still knew barely anything despite speaking again to John the previous evening. He'd backtracked just a little on his original grim announcement; having found out more, he now assured me they didn't have *too* many serious behavioural problems. They were just two frightened kids, who, for no fault of their own, were going to have to be taken away from their parents. I couldn't begin to imagine the circumstances – and there were just too many potential reasons for me to try – but what John had told me (well, as far as he'd been made aware, anyway) was that they simply couldn't cope with taking care of them.

So sad, yet, tragically, so common. I breathed deeply, my eyes taking in all the violets, pinks and yellows – and, as I made an impromptu shopping list for Mike to take to the supermarket for me, I could only wonder, and hope, that things would be addressed sufficiently that at some point those parents could have them back.

This was central to what we did – we tried to provide hope for the future. Hope that either families would be reunited or, if that wasn't possible, that the children concerned could at least be equipped with some life skills to get them through, and then hopefully placed permanently, with carers who'd give them a fighting chance of happiness.

Bob was bounding around the lawn as I sat and philosophised, and seeing him brought a smile to my face. They'd love our dog; no-one could fail to, because he had such a lovely temperament. Kieron had sprung him on us all, out of the blue, almost two years back. He'd been languishing in a rescue centre, abandoned and unwanted. I grinned to myself. Rescuing waifs and strays seemed to be a Watson family trait.

'You done yet?' It was Mike, come to join me in the garden. 'Only, if I'm going to get there and back before these little ones arrive, I'd better scoot.' He surveyed the list I passed him with growing consternation. 'Bloody hell, love! You sure we need all this lot? We don't even know the kinds of foods they like yet. Wouldn't it be better to hold off on some of this until they've got here?'

'Mike, *all* kids like that stuff,' I answered. 'And don't stress me, not today.'

He gave a mock salute. 'As you wish, Your Majesty.'

'And hurry,' I chided, grinning. 'We haven't got all day!'

As it turned out, we had barely an hour before the car drew up outside, only moments after Mike had returned, laden with bulging supermarket carrier bags. The cupboards had been pretty bare, what with us being away, so it had been a mad rush to get everything put away. Mindful of how scared the children would be, I shooed both Kieron and Bob back out into the garden, so they could meet the whole clan in less intimidating stages – Riley and her partner David wouldn't stop by with Levi till tomorrow, so the kids would have a chance to settle in and get to know their new temporary home first.

Mike went outside to greet them and to help them with their stuff – our last child had had about half a dozen cases – while I finished pulling cups out of the kitchen cupboards. By the time I'd returned to the hall, he was already back, however, clutching just the one small suitcase and a bin liner. The children themselves were following along behind him, with a man and a woman, the latter being Anna, I imagined.

Finally they were all gathered on the doorstep in a huddle.

At which point, I should have ushered them all immediately in, but even I – and I have seen a *lot* in my time – had to take a second, just to process the sight of them.

John had been wrong. The word 'neglect' didn't cover it. These poor little ones looked feral. I took in filth – so much filth that it almost looked tattooed on their scraggy limbs – matted hair, almost in dreadlocks, and rags, in the main, for clothes. Their expressions were wide-eyed and terrified and hollow, and they clung to their carers like baby monkeys to a mother; even as I watched the man try to disentangle himself from the boy, I could see just how tightly the gnarled brown hands gripped on.

The smell hit me next. It was so fetid as to be indescribable, and it was all I could do not to cover my mouth with my hand. You can read Dickens, watch Dickens and visualise his descriptions, but these children, looking every inch like kids from a Dickensian orphanage, smelled bad in a way I'd never before imagined.

But the thing that most struck me, as I smiled my best smile and welcomed them inside, was the head lice they had in their hair. I'd seen lots of head lice, at the school where I used to work. And like most mums, I'd deloused my own from time to time. But these were lice like I'd never seen them before. As I leaned down to give the little girl a welcoming cuddle, it hit me. There were so many, and they were so active, that her hair looked alive. The more you gazed on it, the more you saw what a seething mass it was. A virtual lice-metropolis had established there.

No, I thought, again. The word neglect *really* didn't cover it. I glanced at Mike and I knew we were both thinking the same thing. What else were we about to uncover?

Chapter 2

Fighting the need to gag, I ushered everyone inside, pasting a smile on my face, leaning down towards the children, and starting with the usual introductions.

'Now, you must be Olivia,' I gushed, smiling warmly at the frightened little girl. Like her brother, she had dirty-greyish, straggly blonde hair, and such sad, sunken eyes – two huge blue pools in her pale face. 'And you'll be Ashton ...' I went on, smiling at the tousle-headed boy. His hair, I noticed, for all that it was matted around his head, was almost as long as his sister's. He nodded nervously, as he stepped past me into the hall, his whole demeanour suddenly reminding me of a little boy in a Second World War film who's just stepped off a train full of frightened evacuees and is determined to maintain a stiff upper lip. 'You're very welcome,' I finished, grinning broadly at them both. 'Come on,' I said. 'Come in. It's lovely to meet you.'

I straightened again, shocked at how tiny they seemed. So much smaller and younger than the ages ascribed to them. I then turned my attention to the two adults. 'Nice to meet you both,' I said, proffering a hand, which, after disentangling themselves from the children, who were still clutching on to them, the man and the woman shook in turn. 'And this is my husband, Mike,' I finished. Mike duly did likewise, before saying his own cheerful hellos to the little ones, who visibly shrank back at the sound of his voice.

'Great to meet you too,' the female social worker said. 'I wonder … could the children perhaps go and sit down somewhere? Watch some telly or something? You'd like that, wouldn't you?' she added, turning to her two charges. Ashton nodded.

'Of course,' I said, 'Come this way, kids.' I led them both into the living room and switched on the television, flicking through to find a cartoon channel for them to watch. Mike, meanwhile, I could hear, had led the two adults into the dining room, so we could all have a proper briefing over coffee before they left.

The children sat, huddled close to one another on the edge of the sofa, meekly and silently accepting the drinks of squash and biscuits that I'd already prepared in anticipation of their arrival. They looked I thought, a little like extras from *Les Misérables*. I tried not to think about their proximity to my soft furnishings. Head lice can't jump, I reminded myself firmly, as I left them to it and went to join the adults.

Mike was pouring coffees when I walked into the dining room. 'Here we are, love,' he said, handing me my one.

The female social worker smiled across as I took my place at the table. 'I'm Anna,' she said. 'We spoke on the phone. And this is Robert,' she finished. 'Robert Foster.' He raised a hand. 'He's the family support worker attached to the children.'

Mike, the coffees dealt with, now sat down as well. 'So,' he said, 'what can you tell us about these two?'

'Not as much as we'd like,' Anna immediately confessed. 'I've only been working with the family for the last couple of months, you see. The last social worker on the case was involved with the family for six years, or so I'm told, but, regrettably, she's on long-term sick leave right now, so I'm pretty new to the situation. All I *can* tell you is that there are three more children – all of them younger; two, three and four, they are – who were removed and found a placement two months back.

'Five kids!' Mike exclaimed, voicing my own thoughts. They'd been busy.

Anna nodded. 'Indeed, but it's these two, being older than the babies, who are proving problematic for us. Up till now the service has been unable to find anyone willing to take them.'

'Why were they removed?' I asked her. 'I mean, I can see they've been neglected, but is that it? Is that the only reason?'

Both Anna and Robert looked slightly uncomfortable at the question, and it was Robert who now stepped in to answer. 'Mainly,' he said. 'Yes, that's about the size of it.

Gross neglect, quite a number of complaints, from various sources, and the parents, to be frank with you, seem incapable of looking after themselves, let alone five kids. Learning difficulties, both of them. Dad fairly mild but, in the mother's case, really quite severe. So we've been going through the usual channels, of course – there's a court hearing coming up soonish for a full care order, but as the hearing date's got closer, and our investigations more frequent – and also more thorough, of course – it's become increasingly clear that we'd be doing the kids a disservice if we left them with the parents any longer.'

'But why so sudden?' Mike asked him. 'That's what we don't understand. Why now as opposed to after the actual hearing. What's prompted it?'

He was getting to the nub of it. There *must* be a reason. What had they discovered, bar the lice and the stench and the obvious dishevelment, that would prompt them to take the kids so suddenly?

Anna answered. 'Like Robert said, the situation's just deteriorated. And despite several warnings, the mother's not turned things around. We simply couldn't leave them, that was all. She's not been feeding them, washing them, washing their clothes – stuff like that, mainly. And they've been eating out of dustbins and stealing food from other children's lunchboxes in school. We just had to act, basically … well, you've seen for yourselves now, of course.'

I glanced towards the living room. 'Those poor, wretched kids,' I said. 'They just look so sad and scared. This must be awful for them.'

'It has been. It *is*. It was really traumatic taking them.' I saw the anguish in her expression and I believed her. This was probably the least edifying part of her job. No, more than that – it must have been grim for her. 'They were clinging to their mum,' she said. 'Screaming at her to stop us. To help them. Really upsetting ...'

She tailed off, and I could see it was upsetting her now. 'So what about their stuff?' I asked briskly, to change both the tone and the subject. 'They don't seem to have much, even by these kinds of standards.'

'That's it,' Anna said. 'They have nothing. Literally nothing.' She nodded towards the hall. 'I helped pack, so I can tell you, there's nothing of use in there. Couple of sets of disgusting pyjamas, a couple of raggy hoodies and T-shirts – very little else.'

I could feel a wave of sadness wash over the table. Poor, poor children. What desperate straits to be born into.

'So,' Mike said, trying, as I had, to lift the tone again, 'anything else useful you can tell us?

'Well, just about their medication, really,' Anna answered. 'We'll obviously sort everything out paperwork-wise, when we have the pre –' she smiled ruefully. 'Ahem, pre-placement meeting. But in the meantime –'

'Medication?' I asked. 'What medication?' This was news to both of us and it filled me with dismay. Sophia, our last child, had had a rare disorder called Addison's disease, and along with all her other problems, the illness had caused many, many more, as we struggled with a regime of careful nutrition and daily meds, any wobble in which could potentially make her seriously ill. And *had* done, more than once. I shuddered to recall the stress of it. And now again. What on earth was wrong with these ones?

'Oh,' Anna said, colouring slightly. 'Did John not explain? Or maybe I forgot to explain *to* him. Both the kids have been diagnosed as having a form of ADHD. They are absolutely *fine* on their Ritalin,' she was quick to reassure me. 'And they've both had it for today, so you don't need to worry. In fact, it's nothing to worry about in any case, really. Just a tablet each morning and that's all there is to it. They do have a specialist they're under, of course, but they'll be here so short a time that it's not going to be relevant to you. Just a tablet a day, and that's it sorted.'

That the children had ADHD – attention deficit hyperactivity disorder – wasn't really much of a surprise to me. As a behaviour manager in the local comprehensive I'd dealt with plenty of kids in school who were similarly afflicted, and was familiar with the condition and its symptoms, not to mention the action of Ritalin on them – that 'zombie'-type demeanour the drugs seemed to make them have. But, yes, compared to Sophia's Addison's disease, this *was* mild. But I felt my hackles rise, even so. Not relevant to me? *Of course it was relevant*, I thought, *you silly woman*! And fancy just springing something like that on us at the last minute. Did she really forget before? I was doubtful.

'Okay,' I said pointedly, 'but is there anything else we should know?'

'Not really,' she said, seemingly oblivious to my slightly chippy tone. 'Like I was saying, we'll be here the same time tomorrow for what should have been the pre-placement planning. I'll bring all the paperwork, of course and – oh, in the meantime, my boss asked me if I'd give you this.'

She reached into her bag and pulled out a white envelope which, when I opened it, turned out to be stuffed with ten-pound notes.

'What on earth's that?' asked Mike, seeing it and grinning. 'Danger money?'

'It's two hundred pounds,' Anna replied, her own smile somewhat sheepish. 'I know it's a bit irregular, but you're to spend it as you see fit. You know – get anything you think the children need. We're well aware how much stuff you're going to need to get for them, even if it is for a very short while.'

Very irregular, I thought as I pushed back the flap. And it was. The normal procedure was that we'd buy anything our foster children needed, then put in the receipts and justify – very robustly – why we'd needed to spend the money. It would invariably be weeks and sometimes months before we saw it back in our bank account. Yes, this was odd indeed. And it made us both wonder. Why exactly where they trying to butter us up so much? Were they that worried we'd change our minds and reject them?

They needn't have worried. While the social workers said their goodbyes to the children, I took a quick peek at the sorry pile of belongings in the hall. Anna had been right. In the case there were indeed two pairs of manky, torn pyjamas, jumbled up with a couple of T-shirts, the colour of dirty washing-up water, and a couple of broken photo frames, containing pictures of, presumably, their mum, dad and what looked like all five siblings together. In the bin bag there was very little more. A couple more items of clothing that I wouldn't even have used as rags to clean my kitchen floor, an empty baby's feeding bottle and a large undressed doll. It looked like it should have belonged to the bad boy in the *Toy Story* movie; faintly sinister, with half-shorn, matted hair, missing eyeballs and scribbles of ballpoint pen all over its face and body.

'That's Olivia's,' Robert whispered, as he emerged from the living room. 'Loves that doll, apparently. Dad got it for her when she was four. Only toy she has. The other one has nothing.'

'Literally?'

'Yes,' he said, frowning at me. '*Literally.*'

I put the dolly carefully back in the dusty bag. There could hardly have been a more apt metaphor, I thought. And in every sense, as we were soon to find out.

Chapter 3

When Mike and I returned to the living room the children were exactly where we'd left them, but one thing *had* changed – it was the smell. The room reeked now, and I went across to open some windows. These poor kids. It broke my heart to think they could be left to get into such a state.

'Now, then, you two,' I said brightly. 'What would you like to do first? I bet you'd like to see your rooms, wouldn't you? Yes?'

Olivia, her arm looped tightly through Ashton's, looked immediately up at her big brother. Ashton nodded. 'Do we both sleep together?' he asked, shyly. 'Cos we do at Mummy's.'

Mike shook his head. 'No, Ashton,' he said. While you're here you will have a nice big boy's room, and Olivia will have a nice small room all to herself.'

Olivia jumped up so suddenly she startled me. I could see tears springing in her eyes. She looked horrified. 'No, mister!' she said. 'I sleeps wiv my bruvver! I already lost my little bruv and sisters!' Her voice was plaintive. 'An' I need to be looked after!' she finished, sniffing back tears.

I was struck again by how much younger than her six years she looked. I bent down and scooped her straight up into my arms. She was as light as a feather; it felt like I was holding a baby, all the more so when she wrapped both her arms and legs around me, then buried her face in my neck and began sobbing. 'Shhh, sweetie,' I soothed. 'You will love your room, I promise. It's a princess's room, specially for beautiful little girls like you.'

'But, miss,' she sniffled. 'I always piss the bed when I get scareded, an' I *will* be scared, I really, really will!'

'She will, miss,' Ashton added. ''s why we need to sleep together.'

I kissed Olivia's forehead, trying my utmost to keep her wild infested hair from my own, before settling her back down onto the sofa. 'Now, listen, kids,' I said gently. 'First off, you're making me feel like I'm back at school again. It's Mike and Casey, isn't it, Mike?' Mike grinned at them and nodded. 'No Mr and Miss stuff round here. And second, the bedrooms have already been arranged for you.' I turned to Ashton. 'Ashton,' I said, 'At nine, you are practically a grown-up – far too old to be sharing a room with your little sister. She'll be absolutely fine, and we can keep your doors open, and with the landing light on too, so she won't be scared. You don't want to be in a room cluttered with toys and dolls, do you?'

I could have bitten my tongue as soon as heard myself say that. What was I thinking? These kids had never *had* any toys. It must have gone over Ashton's head, though, because he looked thoughtful before saying, 'Yeah, Olivia. I'm fed up with sharing with girls anyway. I wanna proper grown-up boy's room so I can do boy's stuff, okay?'

'Yeah, well!' shouted Olivia, her tears gone, her voice indignant. 'I'm sleeping in a princess room, so there! An' I don't want no smelly boys in it, okay?'

'Well, that's that, then!' laughed Mike. 'Come on, then, kids. What are we waiting for? Let's go and show you round the house!'

But I stopped him. 'Hmm, Mike,' I said. 'I tell you what. Why don't I show them around while you pop down to the chemist's and get some of that special shampoo we used to use on our kids when they were little?' It took a few seconds, but, with the help of my scratching my head somewhat emphatically, it eventually dawned on him what I meant. 'Ah,' he said. 'Good idea! Anything else I need to get while I'm there?'

I was just about to open my mouth, when Olivia piped up. 'Could you get us some stuff for our nits, Mike?' she asked him. 'Anna said you'd get rid of 'em for us.'

While Mike set off to get the head-lice shampoo, I thought it would be a good idea to take the children to meet Kieron and Bob. They were both chilling in the sunshine, Kieron asleep on my sun lounger and the dog, more practically, given his fur, stretched out in the shade under a bush. The children whooped, and immediately ran to pet him, which woke up Kieron, who sat up, still sleepy. He rubbed his eyes for a bit before fixing his gaze on the two little ones and exclaiming, 'What the ...? Oh my *God*, Mum!'

'Hush!' I chided. 'They're not deaf, Kieron, for goodness' sake. And besides, it's just dirt. We'll soon have them cleaned up. Oh, and they have head lice, just to warn you, so not too close, eh?'

He wrinkled his nose in distaste. 'Oh, don't worry. I *won't* be.' But then he jumped up from the sun lounger. 'Hey, you two!' he called. 'How about you come and tell me who you both are, then?'

Ashton shyly introduced himself, once again adopting that rather stiff, formal expression he had when he'd arrived. It was rather endearing, I thought. It was as if he knew he had a responsibility to set a good example for his little sister, by giving a good account of himself. A responsibility he clearly took very seriously.

'An' this is my little sister. She's called Olivia,' he explained. 'But you can probably call her Livs, can't he, Livs?'

He turned to his sister, who was blushing now, under Kieron's smiling scrutiny.

'Can I?' asked Kieron. 'Would that be okay with you?'

Olivia stood and thought for some time before answering. 'Maybe,' she said eventually.

Kieron nodded seriously. 'Well, you just let me know when,' he said. 'Okay?' It was difficult for me to keep a straight face.

Olivia it was, then. For the moment at least. But so far, so good. As they had clearly warmed to Kieron – he was such a sunny personality, it was difficult for anyone not to – I suggested that it was he who led the tour of their new bedrooms, while I went off to phone his sister, Riley. There was no way I was going to put the kids in any of the things that had come with them – they were fit for nowhere but an incinerator – so I needed some clothes for them urgently. And, bless her, Riley said she'd head straight into town and get them two sets of T-shirt and shorts, plus flip-flops, and some underwear to see us through the night. Once they were respectable, of course, I could take them in myself, to choose their own clothes and nightwear, but for now that would do. Thank goodness it was summer.

I joined the party upstairs just as Mike returned with the bug-zapping lotion. It was almost lunchtime but I had a higher priority. To see the lice gone before they infested the whole family. They might not be able to jump but they were very efficient crawlers, and anxious young children needed lots of hugs and cuddles. Not a very practical combination if we wanted to stay nit-free.

'Right,' I said, brandishing my family-sized bottle. 'Time to get you both showered!'

The effect was electric. They both huddled on Olivia's bed. 'What's wrong?' I asked them. 'You need to get in the shower so I can do your heads with my special magic shampoo.'

'We're scared,' Olivia whimpered. 'We don't fink we like showered.'

'There's nothing to be scared of,' said Mike in his best reassuring voice. 'Casey and Kieron and me all have a shower every day. It's lovely. You'll enjoy it. Tell you what –' He gestured towards Ashton. 'Ashton's the eldest, and he's a big boy, so how about he goes first? That way he can show you how easy it all is. Come on Ash!' he said jovially. Ashton looked terrified but, bless him, he got off the bed and followed Mike, albeit very reluctantly, into the bathroom.

Olivia, at this, leapt up and followed the pair of them, huddling nervously behind me in the doorway. Us helping the children shower was unusual in itself. But one of the things Anna had mentioned as an afterthought was that they'd both need quite a lot of help with personal care – washing, hair washing, toileting, teeth cleaning – since they had no idea how to look after themselves. This was something that would have to be written into the safe-care agreement; a document that every carer has created for them and filed, for each different child they look after. It details care specifics such as whether the child is allowed to play outside, whether they are fit to travel alone and so on, and also contains details that cover the carer in the case of any allegations, including whether help with personal care is needed, and the specifics of privacy in the child's bedroom.

That this short placement would be quite physical was clearly evident, and I was reminded, as Mike helped Ashton to take his raggy clothes off, that we would need to be sure the document covered that. Then, when he'd done, Mike

turned on the shower and, having checked the temperature, helped Ashton to stand in it. It was only seconds
before the air was filled with a series of piercing screams.
'Arrrgh!' he cried. 'Arrrgh! It really hurts! Get me out!'

Mike had had his back to me, but now he turned around,
his expression grim.

'Grab me a towel, Case,' he said. 'I need to get him out
of there.'

I grabbed one from the pile of clean ones we'd brought
in from the airing cupboard, and it was only as I thrust it at
Mike that I could properly see all the raw sores that covered
Ashton's skinny little body.

I threw the towel over him myself, while Mike turned off
the water, and tried to calm him while gingerly patting him
dry through the fabric. I had never seen anything quite like
it.

'There, there, sweetheart,' I said to him. 'It's okay now.
No shower. Perhaps a bath would be best.'

He nodded, sniffing away his tears. 'I can do a bath,' he
said bravely. It was gut-wrenching. Horrible. How could
these kids be in this state and the social worker have no
idea?

'How long have you had all these nasty sore spots all
over you, sweetie?' I asked him.

He shook his head, his wet hair forming commas on his
brow. 'I dunno. A long time. I dunno. Always?'

* * *

Olivia too was covered in similar sores and scabs, just as we'd anticipated. Scabies, I guessed. Something like that, anyway. We'd have to have a doctor check them out and treat them as soon as possible. Many looked infected and were weeping. It was as grim a sight as I'd seen in a long time, and had particularly upset Kieron, who'd had tears in his eyes when he'd come to see the source of the commotion, while Mike and I had got Ashton out of the shower.

We helped Ashton carefully into the bath and Mike and I tried to gently wash him, between us, while Kieron perched on the loo seat, with Olivia on his lap, trying to stem her increasingly fearful tears.

This was as up close and personal as we'd been as a foster family, and though our modern bathroom no way resembled that Victorian orphanage, I wondered what anyone might make of the scene, should they see it – they could be forgiven for thinking we'd procured these two little ones via time-travel, because they really did look like they belonged in another age. It was hard to believe how much filth and grime came off Ashton that day. We sponged him gently – never scrubbing – but even so, the grisly gnarly scabs kept sloughing off, revealing bright red inflamed skin underneath. It was so pitiful it even made tears well in my own eyes. They'd obviously been living like animals.

This was brought home most forcibly when I tried to clean his battered feet and, taking a good look at them, because they looked so odd, decided Ashton must have webbed toes. It was very rare, but not that rare, so he could well have. 'Mike,' I said, nudging him. 'Take a look at this.'

He did so, peering closely, then said quietly, 'Oh, Case ...' He gently started massaging the webbing between Ashton's big toe and the next one, and we both gasped when a triangle of something plopped into his supporting hand. We both looked at it, horrified. It was dirt! A big grey plug of dirt! A further inspection, which I found difficult to make without gagging, revealed all his toes similarly glued together by solid filth. Mike had to use a toothbrush to remove the disgusting deposits in their entirety, revealing skin between the toes that was completely raw and livid.

Next up was to clear the filth from the bath sides and plug hole, and do Olivia, who was in no better state than her brother. Only then could we properly dry them both – being as gentle as we could – and, finally, put them both in clean clothes. As Riley wouldn't be arriving for at least another hour, I had Kieron achieve this by rummaging in his wardrobe, and finding two of his big T-shirts to put them in.

And so it was, half an hour later, that they were arranged with him at the dining-room table – looking tiny and pink, in their band-name emblazoned T-shirt 'dresses', their hair doused in nit lotion, their bodies in left-over calamine (Levi had recently had chickenpox) – nibbling shyly on toast. I'd made a pile of it and plonked it in the centre of the table. I didn't want to give them more so late, for fear of spoiling their tea.

Kieron, by now, had got over his shock, and seemed keen to entertain them – he'd brought down a big sketch pad and some felt pens – so I took the opportunity to pop into the garden for a cigarette.

Mike was already out there, sitting at the garden table, in the sunshine, with his back to me, his head resting in his hands.

I went over to him and rubbed his shoulder. 'You okay, love?'

He straightened. 'No, not really. God, love, it's appalling. I have never seen anything like that in my life. Well, except perhaps on telly, but – sheesh! I just can't believe the state of them! Can you?' I shook my head. 'I can't believe,' he went on, 'that any mother or father – *particularly* a mother – could allow her own children to get into such a state.'

I sat down and lit my cigarette. 'I know, but, love, it happens. And if she's got learning difficulties, too … But I do know what you mean. It's one thing to see it in the papers or on the news, but, this – having to clean up those kids – I agree. It *is* shocking. It really brings it home.'

In truth, it wasn't perhaps quite as shocking for me as it was for Mike and Kieron. My years in school had given me plenty of insights into the state of kids from some impoverished families. But not like this; this was neglect on a completely different scale.

But at least we'd got them clean, I thought, which was a start. Now it was just a case of doing what we could for them, before passing them all on to their long-term carers. And we could do so much, I thought, putting out my cigarette, and going back inside. And the feeling was endorsed when I went back into the dining room to find them huddled up on either side of Kieron, who was playing a game with them, starting to draw cartoons and having them try to be the first one to guess which characters they were.

It was a fascinating tableau and I watched from the doorway for a while. Ashton – being the eldest – was trying to look cool and disinterested, whereas Olivia, in complete contrast, was rocking back and forth in her excitement, making squealing sounds and chewing on her hand. I watched Kieron gently remove her fist from her mouth and encourage her to try and have a guess.

'It's G … G …' Olivia trilled excitedly. 'Ash, it's G … G …' She reached across and grabbed Ashton's damp hair and tugged on it. Now it was clean, I could see just how long it was. I made a mental note: cherubic though he looked with his now soft and curly locks, I must get it cut as a matter of priority. 'Get off, Livs!' Ashton snapped, clipping his little sister around the head. 'I know who it is, okay? I'm not thick!'

'Hey,' Kieron chided. 'Less of the hitting, okay? That's naughty, Ashton. And well done Olivia! It *is* Garfield. You clever girl, you!'

I was amazed. I couldn't believe my son had understood what on earth she was on about, because I certainly hadn't. I was just about to go in and congratulate Olivia myself, when I heard a key in the lock and saw a shadow through the glass in the front door. It was Riley and Levi, bearing clothing.

Riley smiled at the children, who were studying her warily. 'And who do we have here, then?' she asked the two of them. 'Hey, Levi,' she added. 'Some new friends for you!'

At the mention of the baby, the children's wariness disappeared instantly, and they both got down from the table and clustered round the buggy. Levi, on form, did his new party trick. He was twenty months old now, a proper toddler, and his most fun thing to do was to flap his arms frantically and go 'Hiyah! Hiyah! Hiyah!'

Olivia, particularly, was enchanted, and I was reminded that these kids were probably very used to babies, having lived cheek by jowl, probably, with three of them. 'Hiyah,' she mimicked at him. 'Hiyah, liccle baby! Oh, you're so sweet! Like my dolly! Who's called Polly! Hang on, babes, I'll jus' go get her!'

Olivia sped off upstairs, and Riley laughed as she began pulling carrier bags off the handles of the buggy, so I could inspect the new things she'd got for them both. 'Got some live wires, then, I see!'

And the upbeat tone continued for what remained of the afternoon, the children clearly responding well to both Kieron and Riley. If anything, they seemed more relaxed around our kids than they had been so far with the perhaps more authoritarian figures of me and Mike. Which was no bad thing, I mused, as I left them to it and went into the kitchen to clear the decks for tea, because it meant – if I was lucky – that both my kids would be happy to help out a bit with the pair of them. Which was no small thing. Sophia, who'd been twelve, had had multiple issues, and there had been multiple occasions when she'd clashed with one or more of us. We'd had as many traumatic, stressful times with her as good ones.

This, on the other hand, seemed far less complicated a business. We'd enjoy our short time with these little ones, all of us, as a family. And as Riley had plans to become a foster carer herself, once hers were older, I knew she saw the hands-on experience as useful training.

In the meantime, I needed to feed my new charges, and managed to establish, once I'd worked out that offering them choices was an alien concept, that sausages and beans would be a sensible thing to cook.

'But we can't use these,' Olivia told me, as I handed out their cutlery, just before I dished up. 'We're too liccle for them things. We need spoons.'

And some basic training, I thought silently, as I swapped knives and forks for dessert spoons for today. As of tomorrow, I'd start teaching them some everyday skills. And, boy, was I glad I'd opted not to dress them in their shorts and T-shirts, because even with the cutlery they professed to be used to, I'd never seen children – not those over six months of age, anyway – make such a comprehensive amount of mess in such a short space of time. By the time they had finished eating, half their tea was splattered over them – both their freshly washed hair and their newly scrubbed faces and their T-shirts one horrible sticky mess. The only plus side was that they still needed to have the nit lotion rinsed off, so at least they'd be in the bath again anyway.

As for the dining room, Mike was having to try extremely hard not to laugh his socks off. I'm a stickler for cleaning – borderline obsessive about it, actually – and I could see he was finding this chimps' tea-party hilarious.

'Oh dear,' he laughed wiping the tears from his eyes. 'You're going to have *such* fun with this little lot!'

He was still giggling about it, hours later, in bed. He couldn't stop. And though I kept trying to chastise him, it eventually became infectious. It *was* funny. There was me, Mrs Doubtfire – Mrs Hyperactive Houseproud – and I couldn't have picked a more challenging pair of urchins if I tried. So I laughed along with him. This would be an adventure, I decided. And after the stress of our last foster child, a potentially much less harrowing ride. And they were both of them so sweet, that you couldn't help but want to hug them.

'Rather you than me, love,' Mike qualified, grinning. 'At least till I'm convinced it's definitely *hasta la vista* for the bugs.'

I started itching at the thought, but I drifted off happy. This would be fine. Two sweet innocent children who we could really do some good for.

Little did I know that, so far, we'd seen *nothing*.

Chapter 4

It felt like the middle of the night when I woke up. I didn't know what it was that had woken me, either, only that something had startled me. I wasn't sure what. Had I dreamt it? Imagined it? I reached across to press the light button on my alarm clock. 4 a.m. Maybe one of the kids had got up to use the toilet. I slipped out of bed quietly, so as not to wake Mike.

Once on the landing, tiptoeing quietly, I peeped in to check in Ashton's room. I could hear him snoring gently, so it couldn't have been him. But then I noticed that not only was Olivia's door closed – I had left it open, as promised – but there was a strip of light visible at the bottom.

I pushed against the door softly, conscious that I didn't want to frighten her, and as it began to open so did my mouth. I simply couldn't believe what I was seeing.

She was squatting on the bed, clutching what I realised was an open jar of jam, and met my gaze with huge terrified eyes.

'Olivia?' I said softly, though in incredulous tones. 'What on earth is going on?'

She swiped her fringe from her eyes with a jam-covered hand. There was jam everywhere it seemed, on her face, in her hair, smeared down her front, on the bed. In fact, as I took in the scene I could believe it even less – the whole duvet was covered in food.

'No, lady,' she answered tremulously, scuttling towards the wall and clutching the jar even tighter to her chest. 'I didn't do it. I didn't do anyfink!'

My principal reaction was one of sadness. In any other circumstance it would be one of anger, I knew, but looking at her, crouched in the midst of all this mess, the only thing I felt for her was pity. The bed was in chaos, playing host to an upturned bag of sugar, an open tub of butter and two empty boxes of cereal. There were also God only knew how many empty biscuit wrappers strewn around. She must have already had quite a feast. In fact, it looked, for all the world, like there had been a major eating binge, of the type you often hear about in magazines, illustrating the distressing practice of teenage bulimics. But this was a six-year-old – hardly more than a baby! What had prompted it, I wondered? This was surely not down to hunger. She'd eaten normally during the day and had done nothing to indicate she was starving, yet she'd amassed, and clearly munched her way through, one hell of a lot of food.

It was psychological, clearly. Something to do with her background. From what we knew, and from the scrawny state of them, it was highly likely food was scarce for these children. Perhaps this was a behaviour born out of fear about where the next meal might be coming from. Or perhaps sneaking down for food in the night was the only way she could be sure to get some. Poor little mite. I crossed the room and perched on the end of the bed.

'Olivia, sweetheart,' I said to her gently. 'You mustn't do things like this, love. It's wrong. For one thing, you should be sleeping, and for another, it's, well, it's taking things that don't belong to you, isn't it? Stealing.' She continued to stare at me, as if in a trance. 'Love, were you hungry?' I persisted. 'Was that it?'

Now she shook her head. 'Not hungry, miss. Sorry. I swear to God almighty, I won't do it no more, miss. I promise!'

I couldn't help but raise my eyebrows at her strange choice of words, as I held my arms out to her, beckoning her towards me. 'Come on love,' I said softly, braced for the sticky paws that I knew would soon be wrapped around my neck. 'Come here and let's get you cleaned up, sweetheart. And get this bed straight so you can get back to sleep, eh?'

As I'd anticipated, Olivia let me scoop her into my arms, and after stripping her of her filthy nightwear and scrubbing her down with baby wipes – all of which she now seemed perfectly happy to submit to – I gathered the whole duvet and its contents into a ball, and replaced it with a spare from the airing cupboard. I could sort out the chaos in the morning.

Olivia then scooted meekly back under the clean covers. No point, I decided, in engaging her in further conversation. 'There,' I said simply, bending to plant a kiss on her forehead. 'All tucked up, nice and clean. Now back to sleep, okay?'

She nodded and then obediently closed her eyes for me. But I was wide awake. I barely slept for the remainder of the night. These children were going to be some challenge.

'So did you sleep at all, love?' Mike asked, as I greeted the new day to see – and smell – a steaming mug of coffee being placed on my bedside table. I'd need it, I thought, as I pushed myself up to a sitting position and realised the lateness of the hour.

'Not much.'

'I thought not. So what happened, exactly? She wet the bed? I saw the bedding on the landing.'

I shook my head, and filled Mike in on what had actually happened. 'Not unsurprising,' was his considered opinion, once I'd finished. 'They really do seem like something out of a Dickens novel, don't they?'

I sipped my scalding but oh-so-much-needed coffee and frowned at him. 'And it's our job to haul them back to the 21st century.'

'But not for long,' Mike soothed. 'Anyway, I'll go down and sort the breakfast things, shall I?'

I grinned. 'If you can find any cereal, that is!'

That was the good thing about mornings. A new day, and everything suddenly seemed more manageable. As I gathered both my wits and my dressing gown to face whatever this one held, I could hear the two of them chattering away happily in Olivia's bedroom, and felt my normal positive, can-do mood returning. It was slightly dented, admittedly, when I went in there only to have my nose assaulted by the stench of urine, but common sense told me this was all par for the course. 'Neglect' was such a small word for such a big, wide-ranging, multi-faceted problem. These kids, it was clear, had never been potty trained. But that was something I could easily do for them, starting now.

The TV was blaring away to itself, and the two of them were sitting cross-legged on the floor, busy piecing together a jigsaw. 'C'mon, kids,' I said, stepping over them to go and open up a window. 'Time to tidy that away now and come down for breakfast, okay?'

Olivia, seeing me, leapt up immediately, and tried to cling to me like a baby panda. It was good to see she was so affectionate, I thought, as I scooped her up onto my hip, but rather less good to see – or rather, for it to slowly, damply dawn on me – that she was also wringing wet. And so was I, now. Ashton too, I saw as he also stood up, had a suspicious wet patch all up the back of his night things.

I herded them both into the bathroom, and began stripping Olivia out of her wet things. Ashton, taking my cue, undressed likewise, ready to wash, and though I made an effort not to pay him too much attention as he did so, noticed that he was clearly embarrassed. Now that, at least, was a good thing, I thought to myself. Feeling uncomfortable about bed wetting was at least half the battle. I felt confident I could soon have him dry. In fact perhaps he was dry, and this was just a lapse, due to the trauma of the past couple of days.

Ignoring his damp things completely, I turned to Olivia. 'Did you have an accident?' I asked her gently as I filled the basin. The question was rhetorical – of course she'd had an accident – but her answer still flagged up the extent of the 'neglect'.

'Yesh!' she told me, proudly, as she picked up her sodden pyjama bottoms, gleefully showing me what she obviously considered to be a very impressive stain.

'It's okay, Casey,' Ashton added, in a reassuring tone. 'Don't worry. She'll soon be all dry again.'

Bless him, I thought, as I sponged his sister down, diplomatically leaving him to sort himself out for now.

Once they were both clean and dry, I got them dressed in some of the new clothes Riley had bought for them and we eventually got downstairs for breakfast. True to his word, Mike had everything laid out ready, but it soon became evident that neither of them were interested. In fact, by now, they seemed much more interested in winding each other up; punching each other and running around madly, laughing manically for no apparent reason. It was almost as if they had morphed into different children, the shyness of yesterday having completely disappeared. Ashton, particularly, suddenly seemed a different child; one who now delighted in driving his sister mad; pulling her hair and teasing her and generally being a rather bullying big brother, something that would also need addressing.

'Right,' said Mike sternly, in an attempt to regain control. 'Enough of all this. Time to sit up nicely at the table! It's time for breakfast!' But his words fell on completely deaf ears.

Trying to balance the two full bowls of cereal I'd poured, I approached the table and tried myself. 'That's enough!' I snapped, trying to get and hold their attention. But it was hopeless – they just ignored both of us. Perhaps, I decided, I needed to change tack. Perhaps raised voices were something they had got used to simply tuning out. So instead, placing their cereal bowls on the table, I spoke more quietly. 'Fine,' I said. 'This breakfast will be on the table for five minutes. If you haven't sat down and begun eating it quietly by then, I shall assume you don't want it and will take it away, and there'll be nothing more to eat until lunchtime.'

This, thankfully, seemed to work. Finally, two sets of suspicious eyes were on me, and the children, my words having obviously sunk in, climbed onto their chairs, picked up their spoons and started to eat.

It was still like feeding time at the zoo, though. 'My God, Case,' whispered Mike as we stood by the kitchen partition and watched them. 'If they carry on like this, this is going to be a nightmare! I hope they start calming down a bit!'

Shit! I thought suddenly, remembering. 'Mike, their medication! It's the bloody ADHD, all this! They must have to have their tablets first thing – of course!' What with everything, I'd completely forgotten to ask what time of day they needed to take their pills. And now I'd had my answer. *As soon as humanly possible after they wake up!* I hurriedly gave them one each, and made sure they took them, then prayed that they were pretty fast-acting. Because it really was like watching feral children in action. Though they'd picked up their spoons, they were mostly using their hands to eat, shovelling the food in at an alarming rate, and spilling half of it on the floor. They also didn't sit on their chairs, but crouched on them, like chimps, almost as if ready to pounce or flee.

Noticing Olivia's bowl was empty now, I reached to take it from her, but stopped mid-way, as the six-year-old began to growl at me. She raised her hands in front of her, bent her fingers into claws and began hissing at me – it really was something to witness. I was then startled when Ashton banged his fist down on the table. 'No, Livs!' he barked at her. Olivia hung her head and immediately began whimpering, clearly scared. I just couldn't quite believe what I was seeing.

It took an hour for the children to completely calm down. I had tried jigsaws and colouring books, a game of football in the garden … I'd even tried to make a game of them all helping me and Mike to clean up. Nothing had worked, not until the drug had kicked in, upon which the transformation was as sudden as it was huge. I'd seen the effect of Ritalin in school, of course, but never so dramatically as this. And, right now, I couldn't have been more grateful.

The downside, however, was that they were now a bit like zombies; though ready to follow instructions, which was a positive, they were also confused and a bit droopy, with dampened spirits. Theirs must be, I thought sadly, a pretty strong dose. I made a mental note to take the pair of them to see Dr Shackleton; our local doctor had been the family's GP for many years, and was always happy to support us with the children we fostered. Perhaps with support, and the right environment, we might be able to lower it slightly. It would be good to pass them on having made some progress in that regard, at least, even if, in the time-frame we probably had available, something of a big ask.

By now Kieron, who had finished college and was now busy job-hunting, had come downstairs. Now the kids were so much calmer, he was happy to stick around and help Mike to mind them while I went into town with Riley to do a proper shop for them. In time I hoped I'd be able to take them out with me, but for now, while they were still such an unknown quantity, I felt happier leaving them safely indoors. I had to hurry, too, as the social-work team were due later. So it would definitely have to be something of a smash and grab – I just hoped the same wouldn't be happening at home.

Riley and I loved to shop. Always had. In fact, after playing with little Levi, going shopping with my daughter was one of those simple pleasures that I really enjoyed. Whatever the stresses in my life, there was little that couldn't be made a bit better by spending mother-and-daughter quality time with Riley.

And we could certainly shop. In no time at all we had amassed five sets of underwear each, five cold-day outfits, five warm-day outfits, two pairs of new shoes, two coats, two more sets of pyjamas plus two of pairs of novelty children's slippers. We also added more jigsaws, a tub of Lego, a stack of books and two new PlayStation games, the ones we had being too geared to older children. We'd picked up a couple of new dolls for Olivia, too, one with long hair, and one a baby doll that could drink and wet its nappy. It came with a potty, and I thought it might prove useful when it came to potty training – something I clearly needed to address quickly, particularly with Olivia. I'd easily doubled the amount the social worker had given me, but I didn't care. I would be able to claim it back eventually.

'I can't wait to see their little faces,' I told Riley, as we hauled our booty into the boot of my car. Riley neither. 'Can I give Olivia the Baby Born one?' she asked. 'Oh, I used to love mine when I was little!' I nodded, belatedly picturing Mike's face as well, and the expression it would have on it when I told him what I'd spent. But no matter. These children needed a lot more important things than toys – security, routine, love and boundaries, decent discipline – but they needed to play too.

And we were soon to get a stark reminder of just how much they *did* need. Our return, and the opening of all our carrier bags, was greeted not with joy, whoops of delight and barely contained excitement, but instead with blank faces and disinterest. Yes, they were both polite, and said thank you – and to both me and Riley – but as for interest in the toys and games and books we had bought them – there was none. They looked for all the world as if they didn't even want them. Such a sad and dispiriting thing to witness.

The cars rolled up at 2 p.m. as planned, for our promised meeting. Anna and Robert were in the first car, while John, who'd obviously travelled separately, was behind.

By now we'd given the children lunch (happily, now they were dosed up, a much less manic affair than breakfast) and they were sitting in the living room, glued to the TV. So I left them to it, and while Mike organised teas and coffees for everyone, ushered our three guests into the dining area of the kitchen. I smiled to myself as Mike grandly placed the matching milk jug and sugar bowl on the table. I'd only acquired them recently, specifically for the purpose of these meetings, having never been someone who'd have owned such things before. I remembered my mum's comment when she'd first clocked them in my kitchen cupboard. 'Ooh, check you out, Casey!' she'd teased. 'All this posh crockery! You know you've made it when you own a milk jug and sugar bowl! Just don't be getting too big for your boots, now!'

We'd both laughed. We were definitely not a family for airs and graces. But if I was going to be hosting meetings for all these social services professionals, I felt I needed to smarten up my act on the china front a bit. Ironic really, when you thought about what most of the meetings were about.

Hellos all done, and Anna and Robert having formally introduced themselves to John, this one kicked off without any delay. Straight away I could sense a bit of tension in the air, though I had yet to find out what the cause was.

John got started. 'Right, then,' he said. 'Two things I need to know. First, some more background on the family and the situation and, second, the length of the placement. Mike and Casey –' he glanced at us here – 'are a valuable resource on my team and, as I'm sure both of you appreciate, this temporary placement with them is a favour. But one, as I'm sure you know, that we can't extend indefinitely.' Straight to the point, no messing around. That was John. I looked at the other two, now shifting uncomfortably in their seats. I wondered what it was we were about to hear.

'I'll try to answer your questions as honestly as I can, John,' Anna answered. 'I do realise that this is a lifeline you've thrown us, and we appreciate it.' She smiled ruefully at me. 'And we know it's above and beyond the call of duty.' She started shuffling among her pile of paperwork, and pulled out some pages. 'Okay,' she continued. 'So the family first came to our attention some eight years back. At that time Ashton, of course, was the only child. Karen and Kevin Wardhill – the parents – both have learning difficulties, as you know, and apparently Kevin's cousin, Sue, was the one to make a complaint to us, saying that they were neglecting the baby. Forgetting to feed him, going out and leaving him unsupervised – things like that. So we intervened, but the report from the social worker was unequivocal. Ashton was deemed both happy and healthy, and that, therefore, was pretty much that.'

I interrupted. 'But surely, if it was the father's own cousin who was worried ...'

Anna shrugged. 'The report's clear. At that time, her fears were deemed to be unfounded. And you never know what people's motivations are, of course ... But the plot thickened, as they say, because she then went to the police a year later and reported that her cousin – this being Kevin again – had sexually abused her from a young age. This time, of course, the police demanded action. Given her new allegations about her cousin, we agreed it would be prudent to keep a regular eye on both Ashton and any further children.'

'And?' asked Mike.

'And the cousin then retracted the sexual abuse story – I have no information about the circumstances – but we were now, of course, involved. And the seeds had already been sown.'

I thought about how much time had passed – and how many offspring were now involved. This was turning into quite an epic. 'And then what?' I said. 'They had four more children, and you say social services have been involved since Ashton was a baby? So how did we get from there to here?'

Anna cleared her throat. She looked embarrassed. And seeing her expression made me sure that we were about to hear an all too familiar story. But you were damned if you did and damned if you didn't where social work was concerned. 'Robert,' she suggested, 'why don't you run through some of the follow-up reports and recommendations?'

Robert duly plucked a file from his briefcase, which was on the table. 'I know how this will look,' he said, 'when you see it in black and white, but there've been a succession of different social workers attached to the family over the years, each with their own priorities and agendas. In retrospect, it's clearly a family that should have been dealt with a long time ago, but you have to remember –' he looked earnest – 'that our primary aim, always, is to help parents cope. To give them strategies and tools to assist them. The last thing we want is to break up loving families.'

I stared at him incredulously. I'd barely had them two days, and on that evidence I could hardly believe that he believed – or at least, seemed to – that these kids should still be with their parents. Was that what he was saying? 'So why did they come into care, then?' I wanted to know.

'Well, in the end, we realised they *couldn't* cope. They've had several warnings and there've been lots of interventions, but after year after year of evidence, such as them being sent to school unkempt' – I smiled wryly: such a benign word to describe the state of them! – 'and not being fed, running around at all hours of the night ... they were stealing and getting into trouble from a very young age. Eating out of bins, pinching the contents of other children's lunchboxes ... I can obviously leave you a full report to read ... Anyway, the list went on, and we eventually applied for a court order.'

John had been listening to this intently and scribbling notes. 'Ah, the court order. I understand this is still on-going. Is that right?'

'Yes,' Anna confirmed. 'And, um, it's just been adjourned again. The final hearing was supposed to be this week but it seems the parents have a new solicitor who is insisting upon new psychological reports being compiled for both parents, plus the children.'

'Do we know why?' John asked. 'Are they mounting a defence? And what does this mean in terms of looking for a placement?'

'Well, that's the problem, to be honest,' Anna admitted. 'Until it's ruled that the children are officially in the care of the local authority, it's going to be extremely difficult to get a full-time placement for them. If we do that, we are obviously pre-judging the outcome of the final hearing, and the parents' solicitor will have us for that.'

I was a bit lost by now but, thankfully, Mike seemed to understand. 'Hang on a minute,' he said, having been mostly silent up to now. 'So what you are actually saying is that this "short-term" placement – this "interim" place-ment – may, in fact, not be that at all.'

John obviously understood the implications too. 'Yes, Mike,' he said, as he slammed down his pen. 'I think that's *exactly* what Anna is saying. I'm not at all happy about this. To be frank, it feels like we've been duped. Surely you knew this when you contacted me last week?'

Harsh words and apologies began flying around the table then, but, even with one ear on the recriminations and accusations, my other was on the sound of the two little mites in my living room. I could hear them chuckling, presumably at the cartoon they were watching, oblivious of the fact that their future – their stark, uncertain future – was being discussed in the very next room. It seemed clear to me, then. If we didn't keep them, who else would? And when it then came to light – John was nothing if not dogged – that social services had, in fact, been searching for some where to place them for a whole *year*, I realised the enormity of the damage they'd probably already suffered; no wonder the two of them seemed so feral.

I knew then that we *had* to keep them – for as long as was needed. They needed a home and some security; a civilising influence. Why couldn't we be the ones to give them that? I caught Mike's eye then, and I could tell, to my relief, that he felt the same. These poor 'neglected' tots could at least count on us, I thought.

Though I might have thought differently if I'd known what was coming.

Chapter 5

'We come bearing gifts!'

It was a week or so later, and my mum and dad had arrived to see the children. Fostering was always going to be a whole-family occupation, but with the two we had currently (and with the knowledge that they might be with us for a while yet) I felt it doubly important that we get all our close relatives on board. They were happy to get involved – they always had been, from the outset – but I also felt the children could really benefit psychologically from being in the thick of a big, loving, 'normal' sort of family, their own childhoods, so far, having been so barren in that respect.

'Oh, Mum, you shouldn't have,' I said, grinning at the sight of Dad trailing behind her, carrying a big carrier bag from our local toy superstore.

'It's our pleasure,' she said. 'Really, love. We thought we could all do some painting. Give you an hour's break, perhaps,' she added, kissing me.

Olivia, by this time, had come out of the living room to see who'd arrived, and was jumping up and down with glee and asking to be picked up. She was really so much like a toddler, I reflected. 'Nan an' granpa here!' she shrieked delightedly, while Ashton, now in the doorway, smiled shyly.

We all trooped into the kitchen and I set about making a pot of tea for them while the kids pulled them over to the table. Ashton seemed to take to Mum straight away, and pulled a chair up close beside her almost as soon as she sat down. 'Now then, young man,' she said, as Dad placed the bag in front of them. 'Let's see what we've got for you both, shall we?'

Olivia, meanwhile, having now persuaded Dad to pick her up, was busy stroking his hair and kissing his cheek. I kept an eye on her. Privately, I was becoming a little concerned about Olivia, my fostering antennae already twitching. Much as I was pleased to see her – to see both of them – being affectionate with the family (the opposite, sadly, is often true of damaged kids), I had noticed she tended to behave differently around the men. She was so little, yet there was still this definite sense of flirtation; she wouldn't be aware of it – how could she, she was six! – but it was there. It was tangible, and slightly unsettling.

And today was no different. 'Gwandad,' she was asking him. 'Can I sit on your knee? Casey got bony knees so I don't like going on her lap. But can I sit on yours to do the painting?'

Dad laughed, as he settled her instead onto a chair. 'Much easier to paint on your own chair,' he suggested. I smiled to myself. And much less chance of him getting paint all down his trousers. 'Come on,' he said, as Mum began opening up the pots they'd bought. 'What shall we paint? How about a picture of your nice bedroom?'

But Olivia was having none of it. She pestered and pestered, till Dad eventually conceded and let her sit on his lap after all. And before long, the noise level had fallen to a hush, as both children immersed themselves in the task at hand.

Leaving them to it, I turned around to find some biscuits for everyone and pour out Mum and Dad's mugs of tea. But within moments, I heard my dad speaking sternly. 'No, Olivia,' he was saying. 'You mustn't do that. If you don't keep still,' he went on, 'then you'll have to get down.'

'But I was only wiggling for you, Gwandad,' she said, her expression completely guileless. 'Don't you like it when liccle girls wiggle for you?'

Dad looked every bit as horrified as I felt. I rushed across and plucked Olivia from his knees. I could see that he was completely at a loss for words. And with good reason. 'Come on, sweetheart,' I said to a bewildered Olivia. 'Come and sit here by your brother. Granddad's going to have his cup of tea now and it'll be hot.' She pursed her lips now, clearly miffed to have been relocated next to Ashton, then folded her arms on the table and placed her chin on them. 'I miss *my* gwandad,' she said, pouting. 'When can I see him?'

'I don't know, sweetie,' I said. 'But I *will* try to find out.
I know. How about you paint a pretty picture, just for him?
Then Anna could take it to him for you.'

This didn't mollify her. She pulled a face. 'Gwandad
hates Anna. She stoled us from him, an' we're not to tell
her nuffink!' She was becoming quite animated, and I
knew she had my parents' full attention. She certainly had
mine. She lifted her arms now, waggling them to empha-
sise how exasperated she was by this. 'Speshly my special
Gwandad cuddles. It's not right! My poor gwandad don't
have no more liccle girls to wiggle for him. An' he'll be
lonely!'

Her curious form of words was as arresting as ever, but
it was the words themselves that shocked most. I could
sense how uncomfortable Mum and Dad were becoming,
as the import of what she'd said hit home. 'It's okay, love,'
I soothed, stroking her hair. 'It's okay. I'm sure your granddad knows how much you love and miss him. Tell you
what, why don't we leave the painting for a bit, and you and
Ashton go and play in the garden with Bob, while Nan and
Granddad and me have our drinks?

Thankfully, this idea seemed to appeal to Olivia. She
jumped down off the chair and grabbed her brother by the
hand. 'C'mon Ash,' she said. 'Let's go play ball with Bob.'
The two off them then trotted off.

Dad shook his head as he watched them go. 'Dear me,
Casey, love. That was just all so *wrong*. What the bloody
hell was she going on about? Special granddad cuddles?'
He was silent for a moment. We all knew *exactly* what she'd

been going on about. Not the extent or the detail, perhaps, but certainly the implication, and I could see it made my father's flesh creep.

And my mother's, too.

'I wonder what's happened to her?' she said, as I passed her the mug of tea. 'What she's seen …'

'Way too much, by the sound of it, way, way too much,' Dad finished.

'It's just horrible,' Mum said. 'I mean, it's the most natural thing in the world to give little ones cuddles. But when you don't know what they've been through … had done to them …' she shuddered. 'Well, it just makes it all so awkward, doesn't it? I mean, it shouldn't do, should it? But it does.'

What it most did for me, though, was answer my unspoken question. This granddad, if Olivia's innocent comments were based in fact, would appear to have been up to no good. I tried to think if a granddad had been mentioned in any of the reports we'd been given, but I had no recollection of it. I resolved to take another good look later. And to continue to keep a close eye on Olivia. Ashton, too. Just how grim a can of worms had her words inadvertently begun to reveal?

And there was more to come. As we notched up a full second week with the children, I began to realise how knowledgeable they were about their bodies, and how lacking in personal boundaries they were. That they were close was obviously good, but they were physically a bit *too* close, touching one another in inappropriate places, and with what looked like very clear sexual overtones.

It's generally not useful to over-analyse sexual touching in young children. It's normal for little ones to want to explore their *whole* bodies, and to introduce sanctions, or adult notions of sex and propriety, can only result in creating a tension around it, which can lead to emotional problems later on. But these little ones seemed *so* sexual, it was confirming my suspicion that whilst their parents might have neglected them in terms of attending to their needs, someone – this granddad, almost certainly, and others? – had actually been paying them quite a *lot* of attention. Children simply didn't do some of the things these two were doing, not without there being some adult input.

It was to be Lauren, Kieron's girlfriend, who'd get the next piece of tangible evidence of what I was fast believing to be a worrying state of affairs.

Lauren was currently on her summer break from college, where she was studying dance and drama, and was often round at the moment, helping Kieron with his job-hunting. It was the following Tuesday, and the two of them were on the computer, in the living room, trawling the internet while the children were playing on the floor with building bricks. Kieron had come out in the kitchen to get a drink, and the two of us were having a chat about progress, when Lauren appeared in the doorway, looking slightly embarrassed. 'Um, Casey,' she said. 'Can you come back in the living room a second? It's the kids. They're … well …'

She didn't finish her sentence and didn't need to. I could tell by her expression that something weird must be going on.

I put my mug of coffee down and followed her back in, wondering what it was I might find.

I saw Ashton first. He was lying face down on the sofa, on top of Olivia, who was lying face up. Ashton was busy gyrating his torso, as if simulating sex, while his little sister lay, pretty much passively, beneath him, except for the fact that she was doing something else. She was rhythmically patting his bottom.

'Ashton!' I snapped. 'What on earth do you think you're doing? Stop that immediately! Get off your poor sister!' I crossed the room and pulled the two of them up. I then sat them down, side by side, on the settee. 'Now,' I said sternly. 'I need you to tell me what you were doing.'

There was a predictable silence from both for a moment, Ashton looking doggedly at the floor, his shoulders drooping, though little Olivia was grinning from ear to ear. Then she spoke, and at the same time placed her hand inside her shorts. 'We were just tickling our pee pees, that's all.'

I kept my stern face in place, but knelt down to their level. 'Stop that, Olivia,' I said. She pulled her hand back out again. 'We don't do things like that in front of other people, okay, sweetheart? Your body is private,' I explained.

'Yeah,' said Ashton, who'd suddenly become animated, watching her. 'We can only do that in our bedroom, Liv, stop it!' He leaned towards her. 'Remember – walls have ears!'

'An' eyes, too!' she answered, dramatically, gesturing to her own now. 'Sorry, Ash,' she finished. 'I forgetted.'

If the implications of what they were saying hadn't been so awful, their choice of words would have almost sounded comic. As it was, it was chilling, and a picture came immediately to mind: of this 'Gwandad' or whoever, making it clear to these poor mites just how important it was to keep their secret.

'No!' I said, firmly. 'We don't touch people like that at *all*! Not down here, not in your bedrooms, not *anywhere*. Walls *don't* have ears, or eyes, but other people *do*. Other people who know it isn't right to touch others' private parts.'

They both stared at me in utter confusion. Which made it hit home to me even harder. They simply didn't understand me. They so obviously thought what they were doing was normal. Except not quite, as they clearly knew – well, Ashton did, anyway – that the adults close to them wanted it kept a secret.

'Not even family, Casey?' Ashton asked me, quite innocently, as if he was in a classroom asking a teacher a question. 'It's all right if it's family. It doesn't matter if it's family.'

'Yes, it *does* matter, love,' I tried to explain to him. 'Our bodies belong only to us, d'you understand? Which means it's wrong to let someone else touch our private parts. It's wrong of them to do that to you. Even family.'

They both stared at me, two pairs of wide, uncomprehending eyes. They really didn't understand what I was on about. I stood up again, and glanced across at Kieron and Lauren, who were still framed in the doorway, open-mouthed. We exchanged a look that said it all; if it was as entrenched as it appeared, this was going to be a massive thing to deal with. A five-minute chat with them wouldn't even scratch the surface.

Taking my rising as a cue that the lecture was over, the children both got up off the sofa, and began playing with the building blocks again. Whatever they were building, all I could think of was icebergs. And how I'd just got a glance at the great seething mass beneath the tip of this one.

I spent much of the week that followed making notes on the computer, carefully recording every incident I witnessed and reporting it by email to both John and Anna. There was clear evidence here of an even darker family back-ground, and it was vital the authorities know about it, particularly with the hearing coming up. I also recalled the allegation of abuse by their father's cousin. No smoke with-out fire? Maybe so.

But it wasn't just the sexual behaviour that was disturbing. Just as difficult a problem to try and manage was the children's lack of hygiene and their toileting behaviour.

I had already started waging a war on poo, as it had become clear from the start that the first night's bout of bed wetting was by no means a one-off, brought on by stress. It was actually the tip of another iceberg in itself – this one composed mainly of excrement. If my nose had been wrinkling in distaste on Day Two, it was positively beginning to curl up now. The children had clearly not had any sort of potty or toilet training. Ashton just always seemed to poo in his pants, and the little one seemed to have no consistent pattern – so I was soon finding bits of faeces everywhere. There would also be smears of it on the toilet walls, and on the walls of the children's bedrooms – even, on more than one occasion, on my banister. It was sickening and I began to feel nervous about touching anything, not before I'd zapped it with bleach.

And, as with the sexual behaviours, nothing I said seemed to sink in.

'Olivia,' I said to her one day, having taken her by the hand, up to the toilet, so that we could together take a look at what she'd used to decorate the toilet wall. The smell was so intense that I was gagging as I did so, but she seemed completely oblivious. 'Do you know what that is?' I said, pointing. She nodded and smiled.

'Poo!' she said, grinning. 'It's poo! Poo poo poo!'

'That's right,' I said. 'Poo. And now poor Casey has to clean it. And that's not very nice for me, is it?' She looked at me blankly. The concept of 'cleaning' was obviously new to her, and I wondered in what sort of God-awful place she must have lived. 'Look, sweetie,' I said gently, once I'd banished the offending streaks. 'Let me show you how we go to the toilet, okay?'

I took a few sheets of loo roll and held them in front of Olivia. 'After we've done a poo, we take some paper from the roll – like this – then we wipe our bottoms – very carefully – and pop the paper in the toilet. Like this, see?' I then did some acting. It was probably a good thing that no one could see me, because I then took more loo roll, started la la la-ing, as if singing to myself, and proceeded to mime what one did when one had finished on the toilet, wiping the paper across the seat of my trousers in an exaggerated fashion and saying 'pooh!', before depositing the paper in the toilet with a flourish, and pressing the flush with a grand 'ta da!'

Olivia, transfixed, found all this riveting and, like any six-year-old, was keen to play 'pooh!' herself. I let her practise about five times before she tired of it, then took her to the basin, where we then spent a splashy ten minutes practising hand-washing too. I hoped, I just hoped, that if I kept this up long enough, my banisters – my whole house – would thank me.

But it wasn't just a case of learning new skills. Olivia's problems, in this regard, were more disturbing than I'd first thought, as I would find out a couple of days later.

It was evening, and, dinner over, both the children were in the kitchen, busy completing a giant jigsaw with Mike. I'd decided to use the time to change the children's duvet covers – washing and turning around bed linen for them had become one of my new daily chores.

I went into Olivia's room first, and was hit at once by the smell. I was used to bad smells now, but this was something else. It had been a hot afternoon and her windows had been closed, but even by current standards – stale urine, soiled underwear – the stench was both arresting and overpowering. I opened the windows and immediately set about trying to find the source, feeling my irritation rise, even though I knew the poor mites couldn't help it. I was a clean freak, always had been, and living in such fetid squalor was really beginning to get me down. Gritting my teeth, I reminded myself why I took the job in the first place, but I still couldn't help feeling angry at social services. If they knew these kids as well as they should have, they would have known about all this. For them to not brief us fully was just so bloody annoying!

I checked the bed, and then under it, then the wardrobe and chest of drawers. But found nothing. I didn't even know what I was looking for; only that whatever it was, it wouldn't be pleasant. I then began clearing the toys on the floor. And then it hit me, as I passed the book case, that the smell had suddenly become a lot stronger. I put the toys down, and gingerly began pulling books from their shelves. Now the stench was so strong that I actually retched. I almost dropped the books I was holding when I finally found the cause. Hidden behind the books on the bottom shelf, squashed against the wall, were three packages of human stools, loosely wrapped in tissue paper. I backed away, disgusted, and called down to Mike from the landing. 'Love, can you bring Olivia up here a moment, please?'

They were up seconds later, and I gestured to Mike to take a look. He clapped his hand over his mouth and I could see that, like me, he was struggling not to gag. Olivia stood, quaking, in the doorway.

'Why?' I asked her gently. 'Why did you do this, sweetie?' I was genuinely struggling to make sense of it, particularly after the toileting lesson we'd so recently shared.

'I not done it. Me never done it. I didn't, Casey, honest.' She looked terrified.

I crossed the room and put my arm around her. She immediately flung her arms around my waist. 'I think you did, love,' I said. 'But don't worry. We can sort it all out. Don't be scared. We just want to know *why*. It's made your pretty room all smelly, and you don't want that, do you?'

She started crying. 'It's just my poo,' she sobbed. 'That's all. I just wanted to keep it. But I won't do it no more if you don't like it.'

'Sweetheart, poo must be done in the toilet, like I showed you. *Always*. Every time you need to go. You *must* do it in the toilet from now on. Nowhere else, okay? It has germs in, and it could make you sick. Make you very sick. And we don't want that, now, do we?'

She shook her head. 'No.'

'So from now on, when you need to have a poo, where do you go?'

'To the toilet,' she said meekly. 'I promise.'

'I was thinking,' said Mike, half an hour later, the little cache of horrors now disposed of. 'What was that slogan the agency used?'

Olivia, by now, was back playing with her brother. I just hoped what I'd said to her had sunk in. 'You mean the one in the ad?' I said. 'The one on the leaflet I brought home?' I did remember it. And well. I was unlikely to forget it. 'Yes,' I went on. '"Fostering the unfosterable." Why?'

Mike grinned ruefully. 'I think I'm beginning to get what they were on about.'

Chapter 6

The type of fostering Mike and I had originally been trained to do used a system of points and levels to modify behaviour. A child would start on a very low level and earn points every day for completing various tasks, with which they could then buy a range of privileges, such as extra TV time, or a later bedtime. As they progressed through the programme, the tasks would get harder, but, at the same time, the rewards would get bigger too.

This kind of behaviour modification programme was a relatively new development in fostering, and was intended for use with a specific type of child, and it had been made clear that, in the case of the children we had now, it wouldn't be appropriate. Not only would Olivia be unlikely to understand it, but as the children were also to be with us only as an interim measure, there was no point in starting it, even if they *could* make sense of it – and Ashton perhaps could – as they'd be unable to do more than scratch the surface.

But, having spoken to John Fulshaw a few days after the various incidents we'd witnessed, I decided to implement one anyway. And I did so after hearing yet another bombshell. Having brought John up to speed on the various toileting issues, not to mention expressing my concern about all their sexualised behaviours, I had asked – almost as an afterthought, really – how things were going with the court case.

'Ah,' said John. 'Actually, I was getting to that, Casey. I've not long put the phone down to Anna, as it happens. It seems that in the light of your emails about what the children have been doing, social services are requesting a further adjournment so that all this new stuff can be added to their final report.'

This seemed pretty sensible, from social services' point of view. What we'd witnessed, both in terms of physical neglect and the strong possibility that all the kids had been sexually abused, could only strengthen the case for them not being returned. I thought about Olivia's comments about her 'gwandad' and shuddered. But the other implication, and the thing John was obviously braced to tell me, was that an adjournment meant a delay, which meant only one thing.

'So the kids will need to stay with us for even longer than anticipated, then?'

'I'm afraid so,' he admitted. 'In fact, the other thing I have to tell you is that Anna has already been on to the Education Department to see about moving the kids to a primary school close to you for the new term. I believe she's also asked for a full report to be sent on from their old school which, once she's got it, she plans to bring over to discuss with you.'

'Great,' I said. Not so much about having the kids for longer – Mike and I had already crossed that bridge, and we were fine with it. But because, logistically, this would cause a real headache. 'So it's going to be a bloody rush job, then. Brilliant. There's only a fortnight – slightly less – before the start of the autumn term, and I'm going to have a whole set of uniforms, PE kit and so on to go and buy. And try to socialise them too – John, you really have no idea how bad things are. They don't even know how to eat using cutlery! Or dress themselves, or wash themselves – or anything, basically. How the hell am I going to have them ready for a completely new school in two weeks?'

I also thought, but didn't mention, that it wasn't just about the kids. It wasn't just a case of the kids adjusting to a new school, it was how the school would cope with having *them*!

'I know,' John soothed. 'I do appreciate how tough it's going to be. Just stick to the basics – concentrate on the simple stuff. And it might be worth popping down to speak to the school too? You know – you and Mike, just to prepare them.'

Just like that, eh? I almost laughed out loud when I put the phone down. Outside, I could see the pair of them in the garden, playing. Except they weren't playing. All they were really doing was pushing one another around and squealing. They didn't seem to even know *how* to play. Not unless you sat them down and explained every single thing to them. John was right. I didn't know where to start.

So, stuff what I'd been told, I would do this by numbers. Well, stickers on charts, anyway. I set to work.

I made two charts that morning. One for each child. And on each I had written three statements. 1) Today I had a poo in the toilet and wiped my bottom. 2) Today I washed my hands after using the toilet. And 3) Today, I didn't wee anywhere but the toilet. For each successfully completed task, there would be a gold star awarded, and if each child received three stars, they would be given a small chocolate bar.

I found myself wincing slightly as I explained all this to the kids. I knew social services would be tutting in disapproval if they could hear me. Using sugar treats as enticements was an absolute no-no, naturally, but I also knew something else: chocolate works. Anyway, I reasoned, this was surely so much better than the alternative scenario, which social services weren't having to clean up. And they couldn't hear me, could they? So they would be none the wiser. Though I did make a mental note to be extra vigilant where the brushing of teeth was concerned.

I thought that Ashton, given his age, might have been embarrassed at such a chart, but he was just as excited as Olivia was, bless him.

'I bet I win chocolate every day!' he said brightly. 'I'm much better at this stuff than *she* is. And it's good, because if we wipe our bums, the kids in the new school won't call us smelly.'

I had been pleased at how the kids had responded to the news that they were going to a new school. Even at their young age, I sensed they were glad to have a chance of a clean slate. 'No, sweetheart, they won't call you that,' I agreed. 'Is that what they called you in your old school, then?'

'They called me pissy pants,' Olivia chipped in now. 'But I'm not, am I Casey?'

'Yeah you are,' Ashton said. 'You're always pissing yourself.'

At this slight, Olivia proceeded to thump Ashton, kicking him and thumping him, while showering him with a stream of choice obscenities. It was like some sort of default, this automatic physicality. Almost as if they were young animals, who knew no other way to communicate.

I stepped in to untangle the now tumbling mass. 'Whoa, there!' I said. 'Now just stop all this silliness. And "pissy" is a swear word, so we won't be using that. And, no, if you do what's on the chart, you won't get called names any more, which is why we're doing it, okay? You both got that?'

It was over in a flash, as I was beginning to understand now. They both straightened their tops and beamed back happily.

But in reality, it was a tedious process. Each day, between us, Mike, Kieron and I would painstakingly go through the same three routines of how to wash, how to dress, how to brush your teeth properly. And every day it felt, though we were *surely* making progress, that they had forgotten the skills were had taught the day before, and we'd have to go through them all again. It was beginning to feel like *Groundhog Day* in our house; tedious, but absolutely necessary. If they were to have any chance of integrating and making friends in their new school, then we needed to teach them these basics, and fast. But it was slow going; if you left them to their own devices – particularly with the dressing – they'd appear with their clothes on back to front, wearing odd socks, and their shoes invariably on the wrong feet. It really was clear they'd never been taught *anything*.

Anna arrived, bearing the promised school reports, a few days later. And as she warned as she handed the folder over to me, it made for some pretty depressing reading. In fact, it was terrible, really, to think that a school could have all this information to hand, and yet no action appeared to have been taken. The children hadn't even been given formal statements of special educational needs, which really shocked me. They'd only been classed as 'school action plus' which simply meant that because they might be lacking emotionally or intellectually, they needed an extra eye kept on them. Nothing more.

The report then went on to list the obvious: that the kids were always filthy, and infested with head lice, that their clothes were dirty, smelly and un-ironed and often wet with urine. It also noted – as we'd heard at the first meeting – that the children often complained of having had no breakfast, and would often steal from other children's lunchboxes. Pitifully, it was also noted that the kids appeared to be friendless, and that other children refused to sit near them in class. Predictably, it finished by commenting that academically both children were way behind their peers.

I tossed the report back to Anna. 'This is disgusting! Why the hell didn't they do anything if they knew about all this?'

Anna confessed to having as little clue as I did. She tried anyway. 'I think the whole family had been known to the school for years,' she said. 'Two or three generations of them – parents, aunts and cousins. I think they were just classed as one of those unfortunate extended families. Underprivileged, more than anything. Just a bit chaotic. And there was never an issue with attendance for them to feel bound to investigate. One hundred per cent attendance, by all accounts.'

'I'm not surprised!' I almost snorted. 'School must have been like sanctuary – the only place they'd find some food and interaction!'

It beggared belief but, at the same time, it felt all too believable. They turned up every day, just like clockwork, so they weren't truants. Just 'unfortunates'. Not Anna's fault, I know, but still infuriating.

But if I accepted that Anna wasn't personally to blame for the welfare of these children having been overlooked for so long, to the kids themselves, she was very much the enemy. Keen to connect with them before she left, she had me take her in to see them, where they were sitting in their now habitual huddle, on the sofa, flicking listlessly (the effect of that morning's Ritalin) through comics.

At the very sight of her, they bunched up closer together, then proceeded not to answer a single one of her questions – not even her innocent, 'So what are you both reading?' Because to them *she* was the enemy – the lady who came into their home and stole them from their parents. And as we already knew, because Olivia had told us, they'd been told not to speak to her about *anything*.

It was sad, I reflected, as I saw Anna out, that social workers, always filled with the very best of intentions, were invariably seen as the villains by the very kids they were out to help.

Not that the children were entirely without help. Sadly, it was chemical, in the form of the drug Ritalin, but for all that, it *did* help. Without it, I knew they'd be so much worse. They'd been with us for a month now and as we approached the start of a new school term, I felt I was beginning to get to know them both a little better as individuals. As far as the ADHD was concerned, Olivia was clearly the worst affected. I'd known this to be the case anyway, as her prescription was for a higher dose than that of her brother, and I knew if I didn't give her her tablet the minute she was up, her behaviour would become the most unmanageable. I'd also worked out that whereas with Ashton the effects of the drug wore out at around five-thirty, with Olivia, it was more like around four. With this in mind, I'd learned to find something to occupy Olivia at that time, to stop her being destructive while her big brother was still relatively calm. Sometimes Riley would come over and take her for a long walk with Levi, or I would set her some task that would occupy her sufficiently – she loved colouring – just to keep the household calm for that bit longer.

Olivia's behaviour, once the drug left her system, could be bizarre, too. Sometimes she would sit and write the same word, over and over, scribbling furiously away, as if her very life depended on it. I would find countless such lists; of the same girl's name or the same boy's name. Left to her own devices – particularly in bed at night, obviously – the repetitions could be in the thousands. Other times, she'd count things. I was surprised to hear her tell me one morning, that the curtains in her bedroom had 370 pink spots and 262 white spots.

I didn't really understand the psychology of these behaviours, but they had clearly grown up over a period of time, and perhaps provided some sort of emotional outlet.

But as I was to find out in the last days before school time, without that morning pill she was a completely different child. Ritalin is a drug that you're not legally allowed to stock up on, and must order around every two weeks. Realising I was down to my last two tablets, I popped down to the GP's for a repeat prescription, and then straight on to the chemist's to get it filled. I was surprised when the pharmacist told me they were out of stock till Wednesday, but not overly concerned at that point. It was Monday, and I still had one remaining pill for Tuesday, so as long as I went early on the Wednesday and took Olivia with me, I could give her the first of the new batch right away.

Wednesday arrived, and, predictably, Olivia was jumpy without her meds, but as soon as Riley arrived – she'd offered to come and look after Ashton for me – I was able to take her straight to the chemist's. Though that in itself was a trial (just getting her to hold my hand and behave was a mission in itself), it was nothing compared to what was coming; the pills, I was told by the pharmacist when I got there, would not be arriving for two hours!

I tried my best. I asked if perhaps he could let me have just one pill; surely he had one or two knocking around? But he looked at me as if I was stupid. 'She doesn't look *that* bad,' was his opinion, his expression somewhat stern. I left the chemists red-faced, feeling like a drug pusher.

But he was wrong. It was one of the longest two-hour periods of my life. I could only fire-fight, as her behaviour – already on the stressful side of 'difficult' – just seemed to unravel before my eyes.

'Let's go and buy you a new writing book,' I suggested, as I led her towards the main shops; this was something I knew would be tempting.

'No book!' she said. 'Don't want no book! Fuck off, Casey!'

'Now, madam,' I said, conscious of her ever-increasing volume. 'We'll have less of that language, if you don't mind!'

'Fuck OFF!' she said again, this time kicking me hard, for good measure, before wrenching her hand from my grasp and, before I could stop her, sprinting off along the busy pavement.

I gave chase, alarmed to see how easily she barged through all the shoppers, and also conscious that, even from this distance, I could still hear her, as she swore at any obstacle that got in her way.

Luckily, a woman with a pram saw what was happening and, to my great relief, grabbed her and held on tight.

'Oh, I'm so sorry!' I said, as Olivia started kicking *her* now, spitting at her for good measure, and trying to bite her. 'She has ADHD,' I explained. 'And she needs to take her pill ...'

But my saviour had her own ideas about the spectacle she'd become a part of. 'That's no excuse,' she snapped, fielding another shin-kick. 'She needs to be taught some manners, the little brat!'

Never had I been so relieved to get a tablet into Olivia's mouth as I was on that particular Wednesday morning.

Ashton, in contrast, was a little easier to handle, as he'd yet to scale the heights of dysfunctional behaviour his sister had. But where his need for Ritalin wasn't quite as evident as was his sister's, he had problems that were equally in need of addressing. Being nine – two-and-a-half years older than his little sister, even if he didn't look it – his difficulties with basic personal care tasks and hygiene impacted on his life that much more. He was a solemn little soul sometimes, sensitive and anxious, and who knew the depth of his emotional scars? And where Olivia would still be considered 'little' at school, especially with her build and size,

Ashton, I knew, would get no mercy in the playground, and had the potential to be bullied from Day One. And even if he wasn't – I had to put my trust in the local school on that point – I knew he could quickly become friendless and isolated, and no better off than he'd been where he'd come from.

But, new uniforms sorted, packed lunches packed, backpacks ready, and the day to start school soon came around. And the children seemed really quite excited. We'd already been for a quick taster visit two days earlier and while I'd found the school secretary, Barbara, a little bristling and stern, I was pleased that Olivia would start the term in the 'nurture' room – a very small class for little ones who, for one reason or another, were not yet up to spending full days in mainstream classes. Here she'd be assessed, while the records from their old school came through, and have a chance to settle in and make friends. Ashton, meanwhile, would go straight into a class in Year Five, and had seemed happy enough when it came to it, trotting off with his new teacher, his hair neatly divested of most of its cloud of blond curls.

The parting today, however, was still a little fraught, and I was reminded of when my own two were first starting school; the way I had to peel their tiny hands from mine, and how minuscule the furniture all seemed.

'Don't leave me, Casey!' Olivia entreated, as I kissed them both goodbye. 'What if I piss myself?'

No-one but me heard her, thank goodness – a fine start that would be! – and after ticking her off for swearing, I tried to reassure her. 'No, you won't,' I said. 'Remember, you just have to put your hand up, like I showed you.'

I didn't linger. Long experience had proved that to be almost always the best way, and, besides, I was in a hurry; now the schools had gone back, I could enjoy some much needed time with my own daughter.

It seemed so long since I'd spent any proper time with Riley and Levi. Just me and them time, at any rate, without a houseful of kids, so today that was where I headed. Levi was a toddler now, stringing together three-word phrases, and seeming gloriously normal and well adjusted and uncomplicated when set against the two poor mites now in my care. But this was not to be a day for comparisons. I just wanted to spend time with my gorgeous grandson and my daughter and, as night follows day, it was pretty well a given that I'd get stuck into her cleaning for her too. She was now five months' pregnant, and it was taking its toll. So it was a real pleasure to make myself useful.

And it was a pretty productive day; by the time I picked the kids up, I'd had an overdue blitz on my own place as well. Just as well, I thought, one eye on the clock, as I reached school. It had been years since I'd lived around school runs. It would be something I'd have to get used to again.

But it seemed their first day had gone well. I was just standing at the gate, feeling as old as Methuselah compared with all the conspicuously younger mothers, when I heard Olivia's unmistakable tones.

'Casey!' she called excitedly, as she ran across to meet me, Ashton trotting along behind her to keep up. She was hyper, but this time in a wholly appropriate way – the words tumbling over one another as she breathlessly told me all about her day, while I spotted the nurture teacher smiling. She was still full of it once home and busy downing her milk and biscuits, until, out of the blue, she suddenly burst into tears. Even Ashton looked shocked as her whole face scrumpled up and she threw her face, rather dramatically, into her palms.

'You okay, sweetie?' I asked her, concerned.

She shook her head sadly. 'I jus' remembered!' she sobbed. 'I just remembered, Casey! And now I no like her no more!'

'Like who?'

'Like Miss Collinson! Miss Collinson said to anuvver Miss that I was in care. She's a liar!'

I put my arm around her shoulder. 'I don't think Miss Collinson meant to upset you,' I soothed. 'She must just have been letting the other teacher know who you were.'

'But I'm *not* in care! I'm not! There's kids on my street – *they're* in care. They got taken cos their mummy don't love them.'

I was a bit puzzled. Did Olivia not understand that they were being fostered? I pulled a photo album from a shelf in the kitchen and beckoned her to me. Ashton, no longer interested now he knew what had upset her, wandered into the living room and started flicking through the channels on the remote. So he was sorted. I took her with me into the conservatory.

'Look at these,' I said, once we were snuggled on the sofa. 'These are children who've lived with me and Mike for a bit. They were just like you and Ashton – they needed somewhere to stay for a bit, when their mummies couldn't look after them. Nothing to get upset about – it's just staying with someone else for a while.'

Her eyes, by this time, were like saucers. 'Casey, are you a foster mother?' she asked incredulously.

I was just nodding in reply when she leapt from the sofa and rushed indoors. I caught up with her back in the living room. She had her hands on her hips and was shaking her head.

'Guess what, Ash?' she said. 'We're in *care*! That's right! Proper care, like them kids down our street!'

Ashton now looked as wide-eyed as Olivia had. How ridiculous, I fumed, as I tried to explain and to settle them. Why had nobody *told* them? And if they'd made a conscious decision not to, why had nobody thought to tell *us*? I called Anna at the first opportunity to ask her.

'I'm sorry,' she said, 'but we thought it better just to tell them they were going away for a little holiday.'

I couldn't believe it, and neither could Mike when he got home. Like me, he felt strongly that telling them lies was all wrong. 'Don't they think this job is hard enough already?' he wanted to know. 'It's so unprofessional!'

I couldn't agree more. 'And if they thought it best that we break the truth gently to them, later, then they should have let us in on that, too!'

As it was, Olivia was shocked and upset now. As we'd find out very graphically an hour later. We were just clearing away the tea things when we heard her shouting upstairs, and both hurried up to see what was happening.

Her door was open, and she had her back to us, and we both stopped ourselves from startling her. The scene in front of us was bizarre and so sad. She had laid out her dolls – she now had three of them – and her teddy, face down on her bed, the dolls with their dresses pulled up, revealing frilly knickers. Shoulders racked by crying, she was smacking all her 'babies' on their bottoms, yelling furiously at them, as she did so. 'Right!' she was crying, 'that's it, you little bastards! For that, you got to go live with the foster carer woman! I don't love you no more!'

I felt Mike's arm slip around my shoulder as he pulled me gently back, putting a finger to his lips as we both stepped away. We crept quietly back downstairs, but as soon as I was down there I had to rush immediately to the sanctuary of the conservatory, before my emotions finally got the better of me.

Chapter 7

Finding out they were 'in care' upset the children dreadfully, and, perhaps predictably, they felt it must be their fault. No matter how much Mike and I tried to reassure them this wasn't so, they kept coming up with arguments that meant it was.

'It is, Casey,' Ashton told me that evening. 'Granddad told us. He said it all the time. If we didn't keep the house clean, the social worker lady would take us away!'

'Mummy was poorly, see,' Olivia added. 'An' he was right. We was big enough to know better.' Her eyes were red raw from all the crying she'd been doing earlier. 'I wish we'd of knowed how to clean a bit better!' She threw herself into my arms then, sobbing loudly.

'Shh,' I tried to soothe them. 'It's not your fault at *all*. Little girls and boys don't know how to do all that stuff. And that's not why little ones get put into care, anyway. There's always lots of reasons, but they're to do with the grown-ups. You mustn't blame yourselves, okay, because it's *not your fault*.'

Ashton shook his head. 'You're wrong,' he said, and his voice was very firm. 'That's not what the social worker lady said. She told Mummy off for the house being all dirty, I heard her. She said, "You've got enough kids. They should help."'

I felt so sad for them. All these words – all these essentially throw-away little comments – all stacked up and stored and remembered so clearly. I knew I would have a hard time convincing them otherwise.

And I did. They'd now developed a real paranoia about cleaning. Any time I pulled out the mop or the vacuum cleaner, Olivia, particularly, would fly into a blind panic.

'Who comin?' she would cry. 'Who comin', Casey?' Then she'd fling herself against my leg until I could convince her there was no-one coming; no social worker hell-bent on dragging them all away. It was heartbreaking. 'Do it proper, Casey!' She would chant at me. 'Do it nice, else the social will take us!'

In the end, I had to make the difficult decision to do all my bouts of cleaning only when the children were all at school. And it was a pretty grim regime to have to adopt. I truly hated having to not clean at weekends. And the rest of the family, who obviously knew me inside out, found it highly amusing to watch my frustration.

'God, Mum,' said Kieron the following Sunday. 'It's like watching an addict drying out! Take a chill-pill – you can sniff the bleach again tomorrow!'

I smiled, of course, but, actually, I didn't find it funny. Even less so when I overheard Mike on the phone to Riley. 'Honestly,' he was saying, 'she reminds me of Monica from *Friends*. And it's crazy because the house will stay fine in any case, because none of us dare move anything anyway!'

God, I thought, slinking away. Was I really that much of a tyrant? They were right, though. Come Monday I felt like I had a new lease of life. Perhaps abstinence was good for a clean-junkie like me because once the children were both in school again I set to with a vengeance. I don't think I'd enjoyed a bout of housework so much in years.

But where we'd at least sorted the matter of the kids' anxiety about 'the social', there was a dark strand of behaviour now increasing instead. Good as it was to have the children becoming settled, it seemed the more at home they felt, the more they felt able to be themselves. And in this case, it meant some pretty worrying behaviours. They would come home from school and get changed – all very normal. But then, sitting at dinner or watching TV, they would think nothing of reaching out and grabbing one another's genitals, or indeed, putting their hands down their pants and touching their own. And when I tried to put a stop to it, I always got the same confused look. It was almost as if they were angry at me too; frustrated that I couldn't seem to understand.

One day, after I'd told Olivia not to touch Ashton 'down there', she grabbed him by the hand, shook her head in my direction, and said, 'C'mon, Ash, let's go to my room to do it.'

Talking seeming futile, my words falling on deaf ears, I just picked Olivia up and took her out to play in the garden. I was at a real loss to know what to do with them.

I wasn't surprised, therefore, when a week or so later I got a concerned phone call from a fellow foster carer, Mandy Ellison. She worked for the same agency as we did and was caring for the three youngest siblings. If I had my work cut out, so did she.

'I'm sorry to disturb you, Casey,' she said, 'but I didn't know who else to phone.'

'What is it?' I said, instantly alert to her anxious tone.

'Well, I just wondered how you were getting on with your two. My little ones ... well, the only way I can describe it is that they keep, well ... simulating sex with each other ... and I wondered if yours were doing the same. The implications ... well, you know what I mean, don't you?'

I was horrified. Her three were only babies! Two, three and five, as far as I could remember. How on earth could they have learned to do such things? But in my head, I immediately answered my own question. There was basically only one way of doing that, wasn't there? The implications, as Mandy, said, were clear.

'Do what I'm doing,' I advised her, once I'd confirmed what mine were up to. 'Pass everything on to John Fulshaw. We both need to push this. There's clearly a jigsaw taking shape here, and someone needs to be putting the pieces together.'

But if I was shocked by what I'd seen from the kids so far, I was about to find out they could take the shock factor to a whole other level. A few days after taking the phone call from Mandy, I was in the kitchen, dishing up tea for the family, and chatting to Lauren, Kieron's girlfriend.

'They've settled so well, Casey,' she was telling me, as she helped me dish up. 'You must feel so good about how much they've changed since they came here.'

I smiled at Lauren but took a moment before answering. In my own mind, we hadn't really accomplished much at all. It always surprised me when people noticed changes in kids in our care. But perhaps that was because we saw them every day, so it wasn't so obvious to us.

'Well, I suppose they *are* calmer,' I agreed. 'But it's still a struggle most days …

'No,' Lauren said, mashing the potatoes. 'Trust me. They *have* changed.'

Reassured, I handed plates out – an enormous roast dinner. One thing, I conceded, was that they were really good eaters. No fads about veg, no 'I'm not going to eat that'. I suppose that, having been so hungry for so long, all food was good food to these two.

But I was abruptly reminded that food wasn't the main issue, as was Lauren.

'You all right, Olivia?' I said, noticing she was playing with her food, and not tucking in with her usual gusto.

She shook her head, but said nothing.

'Something happen at school?' I asked her gently.

She shook his head again. 'No. It was Ashton,' she eventually answered, sticking her lower lip out. 'He's *mean*. I give him his go with his pee pee okay, then he tells me I don't get *my* go.'

I was instantly alert for what might come next in this tale. As were the rest of the adults. Conversation ground to a halt.

'Your go?' I asked her.

'Yeah,' she said. 'It's not fair!'

I turned to her brother. 'Ashton,' I said. 'Can you enlighten me?'

He sighed a world-weary sigh. 'She's talking about this morning, that's all.'

'This morning?'

He turned to his sister now. 'Livs, why you splitting on me? I told you this *morning*! I overslept, okay? You can have your go tonight. Like I told you!' He gave her a stern glare. I glanced across the table, hardly daring to enquire further, because looking around the table I didn't like what I saw. Kieron's expression, particularly, was now one of horror.

'Yeah,' Olivia went on, as if squabbling over a board game. 'Yeah, you *say* you will, but I *know* you. You'll jus' make me do *you* again, like you always do.'

'No, I won't,' Ashton protested, his expression as sulky as hers was. 'Now stop moaning. Just shut up and eat your tea.'

A second glance around the table confirmed what I'd expected. That while the children continued bickering irritably between themselves, the colour had drained from my whole family's faces. Mike caught my eye, his expression one of mortification.

I put down my knife and fork. 'Ashton,' I said. 'Is this true?'

'What?' he said, almost as if he'd moved on to a new topic, and wasn't sure what I was on about. Then the penny dropped. 'Oh, yeah. Yeah,' he said, realising. 'But I will do her, honest. I promise.'

I heard Lauren's voice – a whisper. 'Oh. My. *God*,' she was mouthing. 'Oh my GOD.'

Later, I probed further and found out some more. It wasn't hard. These two seemed as happy to talk about touching each other sexually as they would be about discussing the rules of a parlour game. Which, it was becoming horribly apparent, was exactly how they did see it; as something they just did, to have fun.

I remained silent through the telling – the matter-of-fact recounting, by Ashton, that despite what I'd told them about touching one another, they still played with each other's 'pee pees' when they got up most mornings. It was family, he said again. So it was *fine*. Only today he was in a hurry and didn't want to miss breakfast, meaning Olivia, as she'd complained, missed her 'go'. In fact, so mortified was I that when I put them both to bed, my need to get into the garden wasn't just about having a cigarette – I physically needed a good lungful of fresh air. And it seemed Mike felt the same. He was already out there.

'These kids have been badly abused, Case,' he said. 'It couldn't be more obvious. This stuff is learned. They've learned it from some *bastard* member of their so-called "family".' Mike rarely swore, but when he did, he really meant it. Once again I thought of the all-powerful seeming character of 'Gwandad'. What sort of monster might he be?

I agreed with Mike. 'They need some help. They badly need to get some counselling. This needs action. It's been way too long without any, as it is.'

But it looked like it would be a bit longer. When I spoke to John the following morning, his first question, as expected, was whether I'd asked them any leading questions. In our role as foster carers it was an important central tenet that we did not take on the role of counsellors ourselves or, as would be the case if we initiated certain conversations, did anything that could be construed as 'leading' the children's thinking; getting them to say things which might be untrue. Instead, we were trained to use 'active listening', and, rather than use leading questions when a child began to disclose something, use phrases such as 'And then what?', or 'How did that make you feel?' Neutrality was key; we must remain opinion-free.

I reassured him that I hadn't 'led' any of what they'd told me. 'Okay,' he said. 'I'll get straight on to Anna. See if we can get her up to you for a visit. God,' he said, his sigh heavy. 'It really doesn't bear thinking about. Doesn't matter how many years you do this job, does it? It still sickens me to the core when I hear something like this.'

As I put the phone down, I mentally put the statement on its head. It would be pretty damned sickening if it *didn't*.

Anna phoned the following morning, and seemed particularly animated. It seemed she had some info of her own to impart.

'I have found a file,' she told me, once we'd exchanged our expressions of dismay at the latest developments, 'which will shed a bit of light on all this. But let's not discuss it now. I'll come at around one, if that's okay with you? I'll bring it with me and we can go through it all then.'

Riley, who was over with Levi, had her sceptical face on. 'Is there a pattern here, d'you think, Mum,' she said, 'with all these kids you foster? It seems they hand them over, promising they've told you everything they know, then you and Dad find something out and, suddenly, it's like "Ah, but as it happens, we *do* know more!"'

I couldn't have agreed more. That was exactly what it seemed like. I couldn't wait for one o'clock to come around.

'Eventful week, then?' Anna asked, as we sat down at the dining-room table, leaving Riley and Levi outside enjoying the September sunshine.

'You could say that,' I answered wryly, 'what with the ADHD, the wetting, the soiling, and now this endless sexual stuff they're up to.'

Anna smiled encouragingly. 'But you know, Casey, you and Mike are doing an absolutely *brilliant* job, you really are. And all this stuff you're recording is really going to help our case. It's clearly imperative these kids aren't returned to their family, and this constitutes some solid further evidence. In fact, because none of them have been in care before, what we have now is the best assessment possible. If they hadn't found a place with you – been put in children's homes instead – I doubt we'd have *any* of this stuff.'

So that was alright, then. 'Well, that's all well and good,' I said. 'But my priority is, How do we actually deal with it? I'm obviously thinking sexual abuse, as I don't doubt you are, but as I'm not allowed to lead them to speak about it, I can't help them, can I? So what do you suggest we do next?'

Anna nodded again. 'I take your point, Casey. And I guess all we can hope for is that they continue to feel safe here. That, well, the more comfortable they get, the more inclined they'll be to talk. We really just have to wait it out, I'm afraid.'

'They can't get counselling?' My head was reeling. Just have to *wait it out*?

'We *are* looking into that,' she promised, still managing to make the likelihood sound distinctly *un*promising. 'Particularly in light of my new information.'

Ah, I thought. Finally. 'So what new information do you have?'

It turned out that a new file had been put with an old file. Some mix-up when some papers were being cross-referenced, which led to a possibly pivotal bit of info being stashed in some archive, unread. So what was new? The paper documented an incident a couple of years back, when

Olivia was four, when she'd complained of being 'sore down below'. When questioned by the nursery teacher to whom she'd made the comment, she said it was because her Uncle Petie 'raped' her.

Given her age, she was asked what she took the word 'rape' to mean, and she described the act of oral sex, both performed *on* and *by* her. By this time, my dander was good and up. 'God! So what happened?'

'Well, obviously, we were called in, as were the police. She was taken to a special unit to give video evidence using dolls, but once there she was so frightened that she apparently refused to speak. So nothing further was done, bar the whole family being classified as "at risk".'

I felt sick. Was this the way it worked, then? That if a child couldn't bring themselves to speak about a crime, that crime was treated as having not been committed? 'I'm sorry, Anna,' I said. 'But I just can't get my head around this. Nothing was done? Nothing at all?'

'Nothing anyone could do, not without Olivia talking about it. And that's why it's so important' – she leaned towards me, her expression earnest – 'that you record *everything* the children say verbatim. We can't afford to miss another opportunity to get to the truth, can we?'

I couldn't help feeling cynical. And wondering why the intervening period hadn't seen a similar level of determination. 'And the uncle?' I asked. 'Where is he now?'

'Well, he was 15 at the time, and apparently living with the family. Along with – she checked the papers – ten cats, a couple of dogs, rabbits and God knows what kind of vermin. Honestly, Casey, I've been in there – it's disgusting. Dog muck everywhere, maggots crawling over all the surfaces, pee and human excrement all over the carpets …' All of which, to my mind, was old news. This was altogether *so* much worse. 'Anyway, he's not there now, by all accounts,' she went on. 'He's apparently now living in a flat with some other cousins. And causing havoc on the streets, apparently.'

And on the bodies and psyches of other defenceless little girls?

After Anna had gone, I stood at the kitchen window for some time, just watching my daughter and grandson playing in the garden. What a lottery life was. What decreed the circumstances a baby was born into? What roll of the celestial dice saw to it that those poor children, currently residing in our family, ended up in such a hell hole as the one just described?

I went out into the garden to join them, and swept a giggling Levi up into my arms. I didn't know. Would never know, I thought, as I kissed him. I just silently thanked God for our own lives.

Chapter 8

It was a Saturday afternoon, towards the end of September, and Mike and Kieron had both gone to football. And as Riley was due over with Levi for a couple of hours, I'd set up the laptops for the children in the dining room, so the two of us could natter in peace.

We'd bought the laptops a while back with foster kids in mind. And these two, though woefully behind with their school work, were both really competent where computers were concerned, and really loved the treat of spending time on them. I rationed it, of course, and kept an eye on what they did; Ashton invariably plumping for fast-paced adventure games and Olivia opting for sites about musicals and pop music, both of which, even at her age, she was mad about.

'Just look at them, Mum,' Riley commented, when she arrived. 'You'd hardly believe they're the same kids!'

I looked across to the dining room, where they were quietly engrossed, and reflected that, in some ways, Riley was right. But then, she wasn't up to speed with all the 'touchy-feely' stuff, was she?

'In some ways,' I agreed, as she heaved Levi from his pram and passed him to me. 'If you mean that they're quieter, then, yes, I think they are. But in other departments ...'

'What?' she said, following me into the kitchen.

'In other departments, they are actually getting worse.'

Riley went to make us drinks while I pulled out some toys for Levi. He was 18 months old now, and one of his favourite things to play with was a plastic clock with colourful numbers and moveable hands. I sat him in his highchair, and moved him closer to the kitchen table.

'They're running me ragged, to be honest,' I admitted as I made the clock 'tick' by turning the hands. 'I really feel like I need eyes in the back of my head. And a spare pair for the sides, as well!'

I explained to Riley about all the sexual revelations. About how the children seemed unable to keep their hands off one another. 'Honestly,' I told her, 'it's chilling. I've lost count of the number of times I've caught Ashton patting Olivia's bottom. It's like he's a dirty old man; and she responds that way, too. "Ooh, you cheeky bugger!" she'll go. And she's six!'

Riley winced as she passed me my coffee. 'So where d'you start? How do you deal with something like that?'

I was about to answer – with the comment that I really wished I knew – when I glanced across at the kids in the dining room. The downstairs was open plan, which had been a real boon since we'd started fostering. I could see into most of the living space from the kitchen, and what I could see now caught my attention.

Where previously Ashton had been on one side of the table, and Olivia the other, they'd now rearranged themselves so that they were sitting side by side, with the two laptops lined up together. I didn't know where the feeling came from, but I felt it very strongly. Something about this scene just wasn't right.

I put my mug down, and passed Riley the toy clock. 'Hang on a mo,' I said. 'I just need to check on those two.'

I walked across to the dining room, where the children had their backs to me. They were both giggling and pointing at the screen in front of Ashton. 'What're you playing, Ash?' I asked him, as I drew closer. I watched him stiffen. He immediately tried to close the lid on the closest laptop. But he was too late. I could now see perfectly well myself. They were watching a pornographic movie. I reached out to keep the lid up and stared at the scene before me. Two naked women and a man, writhing around on a bed, obviously engaged in sexual activity. 'What the hell are you watching?' I said. 'Ashton, what *is* this?'

The question was instinctive. It was pretty bloody obvious. But did he truly understand what he was doing?

Olivia might not have, but she clearly knew one thing. That this was wrong. That she knew they were being what they were slowly learning to understand as 'naughty'. A new concept for both of them where this sort of thing was concerned. She curled into a ball on her dining chair. 'Bad boy, Ash,' she whispered. 'I tol' you!'

'Ashton,' I said, lowering myself so I could look him in the eye. 'I'm speaking to you. What do you think you're doing?' He remained silent. 'Ashton,' I said softly. 'This isn't a film for children. And I think you know that already, don't you?'

He hung his head and shrugged his shoulders. 'Mummy doesn't mind,' he said, his expression now defensive. '*She* lets us watch it. It's only natural.'

As kept happening with these two, I was struck by his choice of words. *It's only natural.* Such an adult thing to say.

'No, it's not,' I said sternly. 'You shouldn't be watching things like this. Mummy shouldn't have let you. And I absolutely forbid it. Do you understand me?' Now he nodded. 'And that's it for the computers today,' I finished. 'Come on. Out into the garden, please, *now.*'

Olivia, close beside him, but now apparently engrossed in what she was watching on the other laptop, made to move from her chair as well. I placed a hand on her shoulder while her brother scuttled out. Before getting sidetracked by the offerings on her brother's screen, she'd been watching excerpts from the movie *Grease*. One was still playing.

'Much more fun,' I said, sitting down on Ashton's chair, beside her. She nodded, her eyes still on the screen.

'Don't like that porn,' she said. 'It's 'scusting an' wrong.'

I noticed Riley had come in, bearing Levi on her hip. She too sat down, bouncing him on her knee. She'd heard everything.

99

'You're right,' I said, even though I guessed she was just parroting a version of what she'd heard *me* say. But maybe not. Maybe she didn't really relate this to the 'innocent fiddling' she practised at home. 'And I'm *so* surprised Mummy let you watch it. Have you seen it lots?'

She turned to look at me now. 'Only when I have to. We have to watch it with our uncles an' my gwandad sometimes.'

I felt chilled. We *have to watch it*. 'All together?'

She nodded. 'When Mummy goes to the mucky beer pub. She said we was good kids to watch telly wiv the family.'

I nodded too, but I wondered if she really understood what she was saying. 'But you know you shouldn't.'

Another nod. 'I tol' you. I don't like it.'

'And you shouldn't be made to watch it. Not by Mummy, or your granddad. *Or* by Ashton. Okay?'

She looked anxious now. 'But what about my music and my *Grease*? Can't I watch them no more either?'

'Oh, no, love. You can watch *them*. Of course you can. They're fine.'

She smiled. 'Look,' she said, turning her attention back to the laptop in front of her. 'Look, Riley, it's the best.' She deftly moved her finger over the track pad to bring a clip up. 'It's where Sandy starts to grind her butt on Danny, cos she wants to sex him.'

Riley had bought her cup of tea into the room with her. Now she almost spluttered a whole mouthful back out. 'Olivia!' she exclaimed. 'You shouldn't even *know* words like that!'

I reached across and closed the second laptop. 'Right madam,' I said brightly. 'Come on, out into the garden with you too. Enough sitting indoors on computers for one day.' She smiled equally brightly, jumped down and ran off to join her brother while I turned to my daughter, who was stifling a laugh.

'So, there you have it,' I said ruefully. '*That's* what I'm dealing with. And, trust me, it's really not that funny.'

Riley composed herself and we took Levi back into the kitchen. Thank goodness he was still too young to know what had just occurred. 'I'm sorry, Mum,' she said. 'I couldn't help it. I do know it isn't funny. It was just so unexpected. What do you plan to do?'

I shook my head. 'I wish I knew. Right now, I'm just fire-fighting, really. The more we dig, the more odious their home life seems to have been. The evidence is stacking up so plainly. But all I can do – till social services get some counselling support for them, anyway – is just observe it, and log it, and report it, and then sit on it. Honestly, it's driving me up the wall.'

'And I guess you can't really get cross, because they think it's all normal.'

'To a great extent, yes. I mean, Ashton clearly knew watching that movie was subversive. That was obvious. But I'm faced all the time with the underlying problem that they don't think it's wrong, they just know it's wrong *here*. In their own home it's obviously perfectly acceptable. Take the other day, for instance, with Olivia. It's like being sexual's just innate with her.'

'What happened?'

'Oh, just a bit of light lap dancing. After school, this was, and they'd gone up to change out of their uniforms, ready for tea, but when I go up to see why they've not come downstairs – I'd been calling – I go up to find Olivia dressed like a kind of 'Porn Barbie' – lipstick, tiny bra top, the lot – and dancing for Ashton like she works in Stringfellows!' Riley was shaking her head as I sketched out the picture. 'Honestly, you really had to see it to appreciate it,' I told her. 'It was sick, love. Just sick. She was moving like a lap dancer! And of course you straight away wonder where and how she learned to *do* that.'

'And for who?' Riley finished. 'That's the real point.'

'Exactly.'

'So what did you do?'

'Not much. As I say, to these kids, this is *normal*. And you know the worst thing?'

'What?'

'The worst thing is that this sort of thing is happening so often that I can feel myself getting desensitised to it. I sat there and listened to Olivia telling me that not only did she do 'sexy dancing' for her brother, but also various male members of her extended family, and I wasn't shocked. Not half as much as I feel I ought to be, anyway. I feel like I have to keep shaking myself awake – reminding myself just how appalling this all is. Not just the things I'm witnessing, but what it all means. Just what horrors have been inflicted on these children?'

Riley looked thoughtful. 'You're right, Mum. It really isn't funny. It's just *horrible*. That's what it is.'

When Monday came around, I was ready for action. Mulling things over with Riley at the weekend had really fired me up. It was unacceptable to just let this ride. These kids had been deeply psychologically damaged and the sooner their skewed sense of normality was addressed, the more hopeful the outcome for both of them. I was many things, but I wasn't naive. Having such a warped under-standing of all matters sexual would have a profound effect on their characters as adults; just the thought of sweet little Ashton morphing into a predatory, sexually abusing adoles-cent filled me with both horror and rage. Yet the stats were clear; abused kids often became abusing adults. Which was hardly surprising; if you think sex between family members is normal, why wouldn't you be drawn to continue the cycle? Social norms can be a very strong inhibiting force, but, as everyone knows, sexual urges can be stronger. It was so chilling to think how badly damaged these mites might be, but so much more so to think what kind of *adults* they might become, and every day I failed to try and do some-thing about it was a day – to my mind – which was just embedding it deeper. But it seemed my sense of urgency wasn't shared.

Having recorded and logged and filed all my latest observations to John and Anna, I followed up with a phone call to Anna as well. She was due to come the following week, for her next statutory visit, but I didn't want to wait for that to come around. I felt I needed to make it clear *now* how hard this placement was becoming; how much more complex than we'd all thought originally. I also needed her advice on how to handle things effectively – with no specialist training in paediatric psychosexual counselling, I felt I really wasn't up to the job.

Any kind of counselling would be a plus, I explained to her. 'CAMHS,' I suggested. 'Wouldn't they consider doing something? I know the protocols, but surely, given the seriousness of what's been happening ...'

But even as I said it, I knew what Anna's answer would be. I'd had dealings with CAMHS several times before.

'You know that's not going to happen,' Anna answered frankly. 'They won't touch them at the moment, Casey, not till they're permanently placed.'

Frustratingly, this seemed to be set in stone. They had their reasons, of course. CAMHS – which stands for the Child and Adolescent Mental Health Service – work on the principle that if a child is in transition, it isn't helpful to work with them. 'Which is logical,' Anna seemed to feel duty bound to tell me, even though I knew it already. 'If a child makes disclosures and as a result becomes emotionally unstable, then it's obviously imperative they start counselling immediately. And if that counselling is disrupted by a move to a new placement, then the psychological impact can be even more damaging than if they hadn't begun counselling in the first place.' She sighed. 'I'm sure you know as well as I do what it's like. They could move to a new area and wait months for an appointment ...'

'I do realise that,' I said. 'But that's not a lot of help to me. How about some other kind of counselling?'

'I'm sorry,' she said. 'Genuinely. But you know how things are. Budget cuts and so on … too many kids, too little staff. Look, how about I make some calls and see if I can get you some advice at least? Coping strategies, or something. Would that help?'

Coping strategies. *Or something*. No, I thought. Not a lot! I *am* coping. It's the kids that need help here, not me!

But I didn't say that. 'Well, whatever you think is best,' I said instead. 'But *something*. Because right now I feel all I'm really doing is containing them. Trying to keep them away from each other, mostly. Which, seeing as they're siblings, is not only hard, but unnatural.'

'I know,' Anna soothed, not knowing at all, to my mind. 'I know. I *do* understand, Casey. *Poor* you.'

Poor me. Those two words kept me awake half the night. It was action I wanted, not bloody platitudes.

Chapter 9

If I was frustrated by a lack of action on the part of social services, I was anxious to see less of it where the children were concerned. Action of the type I'd been witnessing, at any rate. I found myself constantly following them around. If they went outside to play, I would casually potter in the conservatory, or use it as an excuse to have a cigarette. And all the while, I'd have one eye on whatever it was that they were getting up to. I also started imposing new rules. If they wanted to play on their own in their bedrooms, they must leave the doors open. And if they wanted to play upstairs *together*, then they must play outside their rooms, on the landing.

I felt awful about it – particularly as they wanted to know why I made them do this – but at the same time I felt I had no choice. It felt so unfair, though. These little kids should be able to play freely with one another, just like any other brother and sister would. Instead, they were being policed and I was the one doing it, but I knew I had to do it, for their own good.

Not that I was doing anything more useful than sticking a not-very-sticky Band-Aid over a big oozing cut. I could see it in their eyes every time I sneaked up to see what they were up to. They just thought I was mad. Yes, they did as I asked them, but I could see it was only because they were at heart obedient children, not because they understood why the way they interacted was wrong. Indeed, Olivia, being so young and as a consequence so guileless, was so matter of fact about her horribly sexualised childhood that she regularly took my breath away.

On the Friday morning when Anna was due, I got up early, determined to have a good read through my log, so that I could impress upon her yet again how important I felt it was that we try to press for some counselling to be put in place. It was with this thought in mind that I tiptoed out of my bedroom and crossed the landing, intending to brew a big pot of coffee and enjoy an hour's peace with all my notes.

Olivia's door was open, and right away I could tell she was awake, because I could hear her, chattering away to her dolly. At first I thought I'd leave her to it, but then I heard the word 'gwandad', which, as was becoming usual these days, made me prick up my ears. I stepped closer.

'There,' she was saying, 'now you're a proper pretty Polly. Nice peachy botty now, all nice for Gwandad.'

I shuddered inwardly and pushed open the door.

She was sitting in bed, the doll naked on her lap, the clothes she'd obviously just removed in a pile beside her. 'Morning, love,' I said brightly. 'You're awake early. What are you and Polly up to?'

'Jus' playing bedtimes,' she answered. Her expression was wide-eyed and completely innocent. 'Polly's being me and it's her turn to sleep with Gwandad. So she has to have her dress off, because it's very very itchy. You can't wear itchy clothes when it's your turn to sleep with Gwandad. He don't like things that itch. They make his skin sore. Even jamas,' she added, as if remembering a very important point.

'You know,' I said, keeping my voice conversational, 'little girls really shouldn't sleep with their granddads – specially without pyjamas.' What was I saying? I thought. They shouldn't sleep with them at *all*.

Olivia digested this.

'Why not?' she asked, clearly puzzled at this early morning interrogation.

'Because it's not the same as having hugs. Bedtime's private. Granddads shouldn't even *ask* little girls like you to sleep in their beds. It's –'

'What about daddies, then? Casey, don't you ever even sleep in your daddy's bed?'

The question was straight out of leftfield, and floored me. 'Daddy?' I said. 'D'you mean Mike, love?'

She smiled now, and shook her head. 'No, silly!' she teased. 'I mean your *daddy*!'

'Well, of course not, Olivia,' I said firmly. 'Because that would be wrong too. Mummies and daddies sleep together, and children sleep on their *own*. Daughters definitely don't sleep with their daddies.'

She took this all in with a slight frown, then shrugged. 'That's a shame,' she said matter-of-factly.

'A shame?'

'Yes, cos you'd probly get a new dolly if you did.'

There was little I could say or do in response to Olivia's suggestion, bar do what I had been about to do anyway, so I told her I'd be back when it was time to get up and dressed, and went downstairs to make a coffee as planned. I spent the next half an hour adding this latest encounter to my growing file, and when Mike came down shortly afterwards reiterated what she'd told me and how I was at least to have yet another piece of evidence to support my case.

He looked cynical, however. 'You think Anna's really going to do anything?' he said. 'I won't be holding my breath, for sure.'

He was right. She probably wouldn't. She'd already said her hands were tied, hadn't she? We were helpless and we both knew it. We could only do what we could do.

With my mind so preoccupied I got the kids ready for school on autopilot, and once I'd delivered them there, I went back to my notes. I re-read everything, including all the things I'd said, thinking *balls to your bloody procedures*, as I wrote. It looked so neat, all written up. All so perfect in my tidy handwriting. But no amount of fine calligraphy could disguise the mess the words described.

I took out the reminder of my glum, frustrated mood on my housework, cleaning things, as ever, being the best therapy imaginable, and my mood was lifted further when Kieron phoned. He'd slept over at Lauren's and had had an interview this morning. But with my mind so fixated on my bloody fostering log book, I'd completely forgotten to fret about how he'd be getting on. Though, in hindsight, that might have been a blessing in disguise. I'd have only fretted about that as well.

'You'll never guess, Mum,' he said excitedly. 'I got the job!'

Kieron had been doing a lot of thinking just lately. Though he loved his music – he'd enjoyed every moment of his studies in college – he was also sensible enough to realise that until something concrete took off in that direction, he needed to earn money somehow. And as he'd always fancied working in a caring profession (despite, or perhaps because of, all the things he'd seen as a result of us fostering) he'd been applying for jobs in the youth service and local schools. He'd turned out to have a real affinity with problem children, and now it seemed he'd secured the position that he'd really hoped he'd get, as an outreach worker, supporting troubled youngsters. It was for a couple of hours each weeknight, trying to engage kids in sport. Rugby, and of course his beloved football.

'That's fantastic!' I said, feeling the clouds part after my horrid morning. 'I'm so pleased. You are going to be just brilliant!'

As if on cue, it was just then that the doorbell rang. I said my goodbyes to Kieron and still had the smile stuck on my face as I pocketed my duster and answered the door to Anna.

'You look happy!' she greeted me. 'Take it you had a good week?'

I told her about Kieron's news, but then I had to burst her bubble. I watched her visibly deflate as I explained what had happened with Olivia, and by the time I'd finished, she looked a little like one of the wet rags I used for cleaning.

'Oh dear,' she said.

'Quite,' I agreed. 'He's obviously been sleeping with her regularly. It couldn't be worse, could it?'

I watched her as I spoke and her expression made me brace myself.

'Yes, it could,' she said sorrowfully. 'A lot worse.'

Any hopes of my raised spirits continuing were dashed. 'So,' I asked Anna, 'what can possibly be worse?'

She followed me into the kitchen and I made another jug of coffee. I had a feeling I wouldn't want to know the answer to my question, but it was coming nevertheless.

'Well, I'm not sure this will affect you directly,' she said. 'But because the court case is looming – it's in a week, now, by the way –'

'A week?' I was shocked. Did courts even move so quickly? 'That seems sudden ...'

Anna shook her head. 'Not really. Not in these circumstances. In cases where we're keen to prevent further parental contact, the judges invariably try to get things in black and white as soon as possible. Anyway, we're prepared now. We have almost all the extra reports we needed, so, bar the solicitor coming to chat to the children about what they want, we're pretty much good to go at our end.'

I nodded as I sipped my coffee. We'd already been warned about that meeting. And it wasn't something I was looking forward to. As if these mites could have the first clue what it was they wanted. Well, they probably knew what they wanted, and it wasn't what they needed. So their voices would be heard but it was pretty much a given that they'd also be ignored, even if it was entirely for their own good.

But that was a bridge we'd have to cross when we got to it. Right now I was more interested in the bad news that was coming – contained within the pages inside the ubiquitous buff-coloured file that Anna was currently wrestling out of her briefcase. Funny, I mused, I used to think case files were so exciting; that they were the gateway to learning all sorts of important things about the kids we cared for. Just lately, though, I'd come to view them differently. They just meant bad news. Every time.

'I'm dreading hearing this,' I quipped, trying to speak lightly as she opened it. Her weak answering smile at me spoke volumes.

'So what we did,' she explained, 'was a full trace on the whole family. As per the court's request. We went back years, right into the dim and distant archives. Back to when files and notes were handwritten, in duplicate, and we had things like secretaries, who would store them all away for us.' She grinned ruefully as she said this – a bit of levity before the grim bit? Perhaps so, as the next bit truly *was* grim, though not as shocking to me as Anna might have expected. On the contrary, it began to put everything in place.

Chapter 10

The main finding Anna wanted to share with me concerned Ashton, and the decade-old suggestion that he might have been the product of an incestuous relationship, between his mother, Karen, and her father, the famous 'Gwandad'. She'd become pregnant while in her last term at school, and as she had major learning difficulties, the school alerted social services, who'd made it their business to follow things up. It was during one such visit that the social worker was intercepted by a neighbour who told her there was talk around the estate about the girl being made pregnant by her own dad. Karen's parents, however, had managed to convince the social worker that this was just malicious gossip, and even produced a young 'boyfriend' who owned up to the deed.

As a consequence, this line of investigation was dropped, but, thankfully, the conversation had been recorded by the social worker, which meant that though the paperwork had been buried in the archives, it would now be used as further evidence of things with this family not being 'right'.

For me, of course, it only served to confirm my worst fears about longstanding sexual abuse. Olivia's comment came to mind: *'Casey, do you sleep with your daddy?'* It may not be proven, but it seemed likely that her mother did.

Or *had*, at any rate. Sadness washed over me. These poor children. So damaged, so young. And irreparably? That their sexual behaviour wasn't just copy-cat stuff was the worst of it. It was almost as if they had an animalistic need. I still felt it unlikely that they got any pleasure from it, but it was as if they were frustrated when they couldn't get their sex 'fix'. Could this actually be true? Could such young kids have true sexual urges? It seemed hardly comprehensible, yet it seemed I was witnessing it – day after sordid bloody day. I must – I really must – read up on this sort of thing, I thought. It was so frustrating not knowing what I was dealing with.

I must have been miles away, because Anna cleared her throat. 'D'you see?' she was saying. 'That Ashton might be ...'

'Yes, yes I do,' I said. 'Sorry. And I'm not surprised either. I knew there was something. And that would fit. And I don't doubt there's lots more besides.'

I would have that thought of mine grimly confirmed not much more than a week later, but for now Anna had something else on her mind.

'What we thought might be best,' she explained, 'once the solicitor's made his visit, would be for you to take them away on a little holiday or something. Just get them away from it all; take their minds off what's happening, play it down … you obviously appreciate they all need to know that the court case is going on?'

I nodded. 'That'll be happening anyway, I would have thought. If a man in a suit turns up and starts asking them lots of questions, I suspect "playing it down" won't really be an option, don't you?'

If Anna noticed the sarcasm in my voice, she didn't register it. I jumped up and grabbed my calendar from its hook on the kitchen wall. 'Actually,' I said, 'that will work. It's both Olivia and Ashton's birthdays next week – she'll be seven and he'll be ten – so I could tell them it's a birthday treat for them.'

'Brilliant,' she said. 'Perfect. And we'll obviously sort the finances. I can rush through some allowances so you can get them appropriate clothing, and to go towards paying for the accommodation and so on. So will that work? Is that okay?'

I told her that it would be. 'And the solicitor? Any idea when he wants to come and see the children?'

'Oh, yes!' she said. 'Of course. Hang on. I've got a couple of dates and times somewhere … here we are. How does after school tomorrow suit – around four?'

There's probably no time that's a good time to have to sit down with a stranger and try and convince him to do something he's never going to do. I could only hope that the visit wouldn't traumatise the children so much that it plunged their behaviours – all bar the sex stuff, so improving – back into the dark days of before.

But in the event, it was short if not sweet. The solicitor was a pleasant-looking man, who looked to be in around his mid-50s, and with a manner that suggested – much to my relief – that he had lots of experience of dealing with kids. However, though he was professional and detached, I could see he was finding the whole business as unpalatable as I was.

It was his role to provide a report to the presiding judge that would set out 'the needs and wishes' of all the children, and as they sat, as directed, side by side on the sofa, still in their school uniforms, he explained that it was his job to tell the judge exactly what they both wanted.

'So,' he said gently, directing his attention at Ashton, 'you know that the social workers think perhaps Mummy can't really look after you properly right now, don't you?' He waited, and Ashton nodded glumly. 'Well, you have a right to tell people how you feel about that. So, let's say, shall we, that it *couldn't* be Mummy. Then who, in the whole world, would you most like to look after you?'

'Gwandad!' came Olivia's immediate reply.

Ashton ignored her. 'We need to go *home*,' he said firmly. His expression was stony, but his eyes nevertheless shone with unshed tears. 'My mummy needs me because if I'm not there she won't take her depression tablets, and if she doesn't take them she'll get ill and then might die.'

I looked on – my job was only to sit out of the way and observe – as the man noted everything on a sheet of A4. I could see Ashton's eyes on the growing piece of writing, and could have wept at the hope in his eyes. 'She might die,' he repeated gravely. 'She probly will, mister. If I'm not there to see to her. You have to tell the man that we need to get back now.' He looked earnestly at the solicitor, who acknowledged him with a nod. 'An' tell him,' he finally finished. 'We've learned our lesson.'

If that was terrible to listen to, even worse was Olivia, so distressed when asked again if there was anyone else she might like to live with that she could hardly get any words out at all. She just burst into tears and tried to fling her arms around the man and cuddle him, sobbing, 'I need me gwandad! I need him! Please let me go back!'

She carried on then, through gulping sobs, almost all of what she was mumbling unintelligible, and it broke my heart to watch how Ashton could see this was happening, and that the solicitor wasn't writing down anything that his little sister was now saying. I could tell from his expression how agitated it made him.

The solicitor glanced at me, blushing, and gently prised Olivia from him. 'Do you want to go and sit over there with Casey?' he asked her gently. He looked up at me now, and I beckoned Olivia across. She crawled onto my lap, then, her tiny body trembling.

This seemed to galvanise Ashton. 'Mister,' he said, rising from his place on the sofa and crossing the couple of feet to where there the solicitor sat. 'What she was saying is that when the bad mens come and burn Mummy in her bed, she will die –' He raised his little fist now, and shook it. 'And we won't be there to stop it! Tell him *that!*'

I could have wept.

It was a bit of a mad scramble getting everything for our impromptu trip organized, and a stressful one, too, because I hated doing anything last minute, particularly holidays. Having a child with Asperger's meant change was stressful, period, because Kieron hated it. So, as a family, we took these things slowly. But we were lucky. When Mike told his boss he needed to take a few days leave from work – and also why – he stepped in with a really kind offer. He had a three-bed static caravan in a holiday park down in Wales. Would we like to borrow it, he wondered? As I'd been trawling the internet endlessly, and finding nothing quite right for either us (or our budget), Mike almost bit the poor man's hand off.

But my mood was sombre as I started to make lists of what we needed – these poor, poor children; what would ultimately become of them? I also couldn't get my head round Ashton's probable parentage. What were the implications of *that*? Not only psychologically, but genetically, too? As cans of worms went, this one was as dark and slimy as they came.

But, as ever, Riley was on hand to cheer me up. She agreed that Kieron could go and stay at hers, which put my mind at rest immediately. Yes, he was 20 now, but he was still very much my baby, and I knew I wouldn't relax unless I knew things were calm for him at home, especially as he had a new job to contend with as well. Riley also let me drag her and Levi around town shopping, to get everything from new swimming things to buckets and spades. It really mattered to me that this time away with the children was special. It was only to be for a few days, but in the midst of so much uncertainty, it felt important to concentrate on simple pleasures, and give them the sort of childhood holiday they had probably never had.

Though I had forgotten one important detail. When I collected the children from school a couple of days later, I took the opportunity to pop in and let their teachers know my plans, the idea being that I would explain things more fully to the children on the way home. I hadn't said anything to them yet, as I wanted to keep things low key, so this was really the first time we'd discussed the idea of a holiday.

But the minute they heard the word, they all panicked. 'When?' asked Olivia anxiously, as I herded them to the car. 'Where, Casey? Don't you love us anymore?'

I could have kicked myself. How could I have forgotten that Anna had originally told them *this* was a holiday?

Ashton glared at me as I bundled them into the car. They clearly felt that yet another bad thing was about to happen. 'Let me explain,' I said. 'We are going to go away somewhere nice. All of us. Both of you, plus me and Mike – all of us. To a fun place – somewhere different – just for a few days. There will be swimming pools and playgrounds – maybe even a beach!' They looked blank. 'That's what a holiday is all about. To have fun! And then, when we're done, we all come home again. You understand?' But I might as well have been speaking to them in French. They looked so completely puzzled that as I drove us home I wondered just how empty and barren a life they'd really left. I knew this holiday would be a treat as well as a diversion from the court case, but, as Mike and I would find out when we got there, it proved to be to an extent that took my breath away.

They seemed more cheery once Mike got home, armed with all the details, and we were able to sit at the computer and look at the caravan park's website. It looked as pretty and charming as I'd imagined, and they at last seemed to understand the concept of going there to have fun. I was still staggered. I'd of course come across children who'd never *been* on holiday, due to lack of finances, but never in my life had I had a conversation with a child who didn't know what a holiday even *was*.

Not that Mike was as impressed with my haul of holiday goodies as I was, not least because he had to shoehorn it all into the car two days later, when we at last set off on our great Welsh adventure. 'Oh, stop moaning,' I chastised him. 'Look at their excited little faces!' So he did, and he softened, and I think, just like me, he realised what a big thing this was. For bit by bit, the children *had* become childishly excited. And about something good and wholesome and right, for the first time, perhaps, in their lives.

I had never been to Wales and I was struck by the beauty of the place, not to mention being struck by our complete inability to pronounce any of the Welsh names on the road signs. Every sign said where it was in both English and

Welsh, and as we headed west we enjoyed trying to get our tongues around the latter, which had both the children in stitches. The clear winner was the deliciously tongue-twisting 'archfarchnad', which, when we worked out that it was the Welsh word for 'supermarket', caused great delight, and even our own version of the game 'I went to the shop ...', which the children didn't tire of for miles.

And the caravan park didn't disappoint, either. Beautifully kept, it sat in big rural grounds near the coast, about ten minutes drive from a beautiful beach. On the site were all the attractions I'd promised and more, and the place was bustling with families with young children. It being school time – we were still a couple of weeks from half-term – they were mostly parents and grandparents with little ones, but that was fine, because these little ones were so much younger than their years in so many ways that the lovely atmosphere suited us perfectly.

And the next few days were largely fantastic. For the first time we saw just what these children could become. What they *should* become. Simply children, doing the things children did. We took them horse riding and swimming, and even took a boat out, and altogether enjoyed every minute. In fact, the only reminder of the kids they really were came when we took them to the beach on Day Three.

It was really warm for early autumn, so we decided to take a picnic. No childhood, I'd decided, was properly complete without having a picnic on the beach. So we made up a feast (plenty of sandwiches to get sand in), then bundled them into the car, and drove the couple of miles to the coast. It was only when we were trudging across the sand, fully laden, that Mike noticed the kids were acting strangely. We'd just crossed the dunes, which sat in a long strip between car park and beach, and he was huffing and puffing, anxious now to be freed from his heavy load. As ever, I hadn't exactly packed a 'light' lunch.

'Come on, you two!' he called. 'Stop all that dawdling and get a move on. The flipping tide will have gone out before we get to the water at this rate!'

Olivia and Ashton were holding hands, as well as buckets and spades, and stepping gingerly across the belt of pebbles and sand at the dune's base. I realised they looked nervous and unhappy. 'What's wrong, sweetie?' I asked Olivia, trotting back towards them. To my surprise, she actually looked close to tears.

'We don't like it!' she said, her lip trembling. 'It's all wobbly!'

I stared, shocked. 'It's only sand, love,' I soothed. 'Just sand and pebbles.' And then the penny drooped, as I gazed at their dumbfounded expressions. 'Oh my,' I said, realising the probable truth. 'Haven't you ever been on a beach before?'

They shook their heads. I was astounded. I had obviously accepted that they'd never had a holiday. But not even a day trip? An afternoon? *Nothing*?

It took a good hour to coax them into enjoying it. An hour in which Mike patiently showed them how to make sandcastles – having to first explain that this was just like the sand and water trays they had come across in school;

and that you could play with it in exactly the same way – there was just a lot more of it, that was all. An hour in which he took them to the water's edge and paddled in the foam with them, and persuaded them that it wasn't dangerous to go in up to your knees. And as I sat and watched, it occurred to me what a big thing it was; to them, such a place must have been a scary unknown. All Ashton asked – perhaps as any other young child would – was if there were any sharks, and if so, might they come out of the sea and eat them up?

But the bigger reminder of their past was to come. Just before lunch, Mike showed them how to play 'beds in the sand'. Much to their amusement, he set about digging a shallow hole, which he then had Ashton go and lie down in. Next, he had Olivia use her spade to begin to bury him, covering him entirely with a 'duvet' made of sand, bar his head and neck, while Mike help me set out the picnic.

About five minutes passed – Mike and I had been chatting – when we realised the family adjacent to us were looking our way and pointing. They were camped on the other side of the now 'put to bed' Ashton, and, as Olivia was kneeling on our side, we couldn't see what they were gesturing at.

I smiled, as you do, as I caught the woman's eye, but my friendliness was met by a distinctly stony stare, and another gesture: she told her child, a little boy, to 'come away'.

I was just about to comment to Mike about how rude the woman seemed when he leapt up from the picnic basket, saying an explosive 'What the …!', and proceeded to rush over to where Olivia was digging. Mike had sensibly stationed them several prudent yards from where we were to picnic. For all that having sand in the sandwiches went with the territory, there was a definite limit to how much.

But Mike wasn't smiling, and I was soon to see why. Olivia moved, and it was clear why the woman looked so disgusted. She had not only fashioned a 'duvet' for Ashton, she'd also created an enormous pair of sand boobs, complete with nipples, as well as an oversized penis. The latter stood vertically – a feat of engineering – and, given its location, there was no doubt in the world what it was.

Mike wasted no time in laying waste to all three appendages. We didn't linger long after lunch.

The next day we celebrated the two birthdays. Much as I generally disliked the idea of joint celebrations for children's birthdays, it was the last day before we were heading home to stark reality, and I wanted them both to enjoy their special days while we were still on holiday, so that at least one birthday memory would be a precious one.

There was a clubhouse on site and, after a word with the site manager, we were able to put on a little impromptu party, complete with cakes for both of them and balloons. He'd also suggested, and I agreed, that it might be fun if other parents with small children on site be invited, to make the thing more of an event.

And it was. We had a lovely afternoon, with music and dancing and party games and presents, and everyone sang 'Happy Birthday' twice. We'd brought Olivia's present with us – a new doll's pram plus a set of new baby clothes for her favourite 'Polly' dolly, and explained to Ashton that his main present – a new bike, which really lit his eyes up – was already waiting for him at home, to ride the very next day. He looked so happy and shocked that I wanted to cry right there in front of him, but then his own face clouded and in a whisper he asked me if, after the party, the two of us could go and feed the ducks.

I knew immediately that there was something else going on here, and it was with mixed feelings that I gathered a little plastic bag of bread. I was so pleased he felt close enough to want to share something with me, but at the same time fearful of what that something might be.

Leaving Mike with Olivia, the two of us set off for the duck pond; a pretty place and, I thought, a very inspired idea. What child doesn't like to feed ducks?

Ashton was quiet on the short walk, and I wondered what was going through his mind. The court case, no doubt. Perhaps he wanted to know the outcome, and in a big-brotherly way wanted to spare his sibling and ask me alone.

But what he had to say was really nothing to do with what was happening in court. I felt so sorry for him. He suddenly looked so much older than his years.

'Ashton, love,' I said, as we sat down on the little bench and waited for the ducks to swim over. 'Is there something on your mind?'

He nodded. 'Casey,' he asked, 'can we always live with you?' I was taken aback. This was not at all what I'd expected. Quite the opposite. Both the kids, but especially Ashton, had always been adamant that they wanted to return home. I had to think carefully before answering. It was going to be grim to do it, but I needed to be honest. 'I'm so sorry, sweetheart,' I said. 'But I don't think that's possible. You see, Mike and I are just temporary carers. And that means we only have children for a short time.'

He turned and looked me in the eye, and seemed to be digesting this, his brow furrowed, his expression hard to read. As ever, I reflected that it never got easier; this was one part of what we did that I found really challenging; you gave your heart to these kids, and they trusted in your love. Yet had to leave you, even so. Because that was the nature of our work. To help kids, move them on, then help another. But Ashton's response, when it came, was unexpected. Wasn't even a response, as it turned out.

'Casey,' he said, at length. 'My granddad touches me.' He cast his eyes down momentarily. 'Down there. Down there, where you said people shouldn't.' He had started to cry now. 'An' I don't like it. I hate it.' I folded him into my arms. 'An' Casey?' he went on. He was obviously desperate to get it out now. 'He makes me sex my cousin as well.'

I took a deep, calming breath. It was imperative I say the right thing here. 'Have you told anyone else this?' I asked him.

'Once I did,' he said. 'Once I told my auntie. My little cousin, she don't like me to sex her. She's only little. Like Olivia.'

I could have heaved, I felt so sick. The bastard. The utter *bastard*. I clasped Ashton tighter to me. 'Love, you can tell me anything,' I told him. 'Absolutely anything. But ...' This was important. He *needed* to be clear on this. However hard it was to say so, because I knew he was telling me something he'd probably never told a soul, I had to make sure he understood what I was about to tell him. I took a deep breath. This part didn't get easier, either. It just got worse. 'You know I have to tell Anna about it, don't you?' I said slowly. 'Because it's Anna who can help us make things better.'

It was as if he'd been stung, he pulled away so abruptly. 'No!' he said with vehemence. 'No, no! Not Anna! She's an evil bitch. They *all* are, them social workers!' His expression hardened. 'I'm not telling her *nuffing*!'

The moment was over. He refused to speak again, and I knew he was now regretting having confided in me. Which made me sick to my stomach. All I could do was trudge back with him to Mike and the little ones. My heart ached for him, knowing the pain he must be going through, yet what could I bloody *do*? I felt helpless. Damn the bloody rules I had to abide by!

Chapter 11

The journey back home from Wales was a tense affair. Olivia was obviously oblivious to the atmosphere – chattering away, pointing out the animals we drove past and talking about the pictures she could see in the clouds – but Mike and I were all too well aware how sullen and silent poor Ashton was. Yet we could do absolutely nothing about it. Olivia kept trying to engage him in her games, but he would pretend to be asleep or just ignore her. He was clearly in pain and there was nothing we could do to help him. Not unless he actively wanted our help, anyway. I just didn't know how to make him feel better.

We'd set off early, in order that we'd be back in good time to get the children fed and bathed and ready for school. I wasn't much looking forward to Monday. After the sunny days (literally and emotionally) of our break in Wales, the grim reality felt, in contrast, so much grimmer.

The kids were both asleep when we finally made it home with the sunset, and Mike carried Olivia inside, while I gently shook Ashton awake.

'Gerroff me!' he growled. 'I can take myself in!' His anger was clear, but who was it directed at, I wondered? Me, for mentioning Anna? Himself, for having confided in me? That he was now regretting having done so really upset me. I couldn't know what was going on in his head at that moment, but one thing I did know: that the bonds we had tentatively formed these past weeks were now in real danger of breaking. This was the lad who asked me if he could come and live with Mike and I for ever. Now he could barely stand to have us near him.

After everyone was in and Mike had started running a bath, I took a moment to check the answerphone for messages. Sure enough, there was one from Anna, so I quickly shut the door, realising she might have spilled the beans to the machine.

And I was right. 'Hi, Casey,' she began. 'It's Anna. Just left court, and I'm sure you'll be pleased to hear we won our case. So the kids won't be going back home, ever. But I'll catch up with you properly on Monday. About eleven? Would that work for you? If not, then obviously just text me and we'll rearrange.'

I replaced the receiver. When exactly should we sit the children down and tell them? Not tonight, I thought. Not unless one of them asked me outright. I wouldn't lie. But better, I decided, to leave things till tomorrow. Till I'd had a chance to get some advice on strategy from Anna.

I was just returning to the holdalls and all the washing when Mike called down. 'Love, could you come up here a min?' he asked.

Olivia by now was back downstairs, colouring in a picture at the dining table. I left her to it and headed up the stairs. Mike was in the bathroom, tidying up.

'It's Ashton,' he said, gesturing towards his bedroom door. 'He's insistent he doesn't want any tea and is going to bed.'

And he had, as well. I went in to find him in bed, in his pyjamas, light off and almost certainly feigning sleep. There was no way he could be really, not with the amount of sleeping they'd done on the journey. I sat on the edge of the bed and shook him gently.

'Love,' I said. 'You okay? Hey, you haven't even had tea yet. Bit early for bed, don't you think?'

'Leave me alone,' he said. 'I've got a headache and I don't want no tea.'

'Are you feeling ill?' I asked, instinctively reaching out to place a hand on his forehead to check if he was running a slight temperature.

His recoil from my touch was dramatic. 'Go away!' he burst out. 'You're not my mum! Go away!'

He was trying very hard not to cry and my heart really went out to him. All I wanted to do was scoop him up and cuddle him. He was in so much pain, and I just wanted to try and help take some away. But I knew I mustn't. So instead I just patted him through the duvet, and went back downstairs, only returning a while later to leave a sandwich and a glass of milk beside the bed. There was nothing more I could do for him. Not tonight.

By the morning, however, he seemed brighter. Which should have been reassuring, except that he was *too* bright. Joking with his sister and gobbling down his breakfast, as if he didn't have a care in the world. It was clear his jolly demeanour was too forced. Not good. I'd enough experience to know that what this really represented was the defence barrier he'd now managed to put in place to protect himself. But it was an unsteady barrier that could just as easily come crashing down. Or worse, become so strong as eventually to be impenetrable. That's what had happened to Justin, the first child we'd had. I knew Ashton needed help to come to terms with what had been done to him, but how could we help if he wouldn't let us? I sent him off to school that morning every bit as anxious about him as I'd been when he *had* opened up to me.

As an antidote (or diversion, dose of normality – perhaps all three) I drove straight round to Riley's after the school drop-off. She was now over five months' pregnant, and her bump was swelling nicely, so one of the things I'd been doing over the couple of days before the Wales trip was to dig out some of my loose baggy tops for her.

These she took with an expression of slight derision; I knew she found it amusing that it tickled me to see us sharing clothes. 'What are you like, Mum!' she said, laughing as she riffled through the carrier. 'You know these only fit me because of my big baby belly!'

'Cheek!' I retorted. 'And don't be so quick to mock, young lady. Any more kids and you'll soon be catching me up!'

It felt good to be back on normal ground, joshing with my daughter. And good to be able to cuddle my gorgeous grandson as well. He'd learned a new trick since I'd last seen him, which he was anxious to show me, pulling Riley's top up, kissing her belly and going 'Baby in there! Baby!' I scooped him up, only to be smothered in slurp kisses and sticky fingers, but instead of laughing as I normally did, I felt my eyes spring with tears.

'Mum, what is it?' asked Riley, her voice now full of concern.

'Oh, don't mind me,' I said, brushing them irritably away. 'I'm just feeling a bit emotional. You know, after the court case and everything. I just heard last night – they won.'

'What, the family?' She looked aghast.

I shook my head. 'No, social services. So I've obviously got to tell the kids.' I sighed. 'That they won't be going home again. Ever.' I put a wriggling Levi down and rubbed the unshed tears away. 'I know it's the right thing, but, oh, why is life so bloody unfair? Why can't all kids be happy kids?'

'Oh, Mum,' Riley said. 'You are a softie.' She hugged me. 'They will cope. I know they will. Kids do. And remember, they'll have a chance now – they'll be going to new families, who'll love them. Just keep that in mind, okay? That's what matters.'

She was right, of course. It was just the contrast that kept hitting me. Seeing Riley and Levi, and then thinking about my two. That and the stress of the last few days and weeks. I mentally rolled my sleeves up, enjoyed a delicious bacon sandwich and a cup of coffee, then headed home to tackle the washing before Anna showed.

I'd just finished the domestics and was getting out my journal when the doorbell rang. I glanced at the clock. It was still only twenty to. Obviously champing at the bit, I thought, going into the hall to open the front door. But it wasn't Anna. It was John Fulshaw. 'Oh!' I said.

'Caught you!' he said cheerfully. 'And don't look so horrified. Thought I'd turn up unannounced so I can get to the real truth. See what the house is like when you're not actually expecting me!'

John cheered me up immediately, as was usual. 'You clearly don't know me as well as you think you do,' I said, laughing. 'I'd rather have hives than leave my home a day without a proper clean. But you're right about one thing. I wasn't expecting you. I was expecting Anna ...'

'I know. And I decided to sit in. If that's okay, that is?'

''Course it is,' I said, as he followed me into the kitchen.

'Good. Because I thought it would save you having to tell me about it later. And I also want to know what our sainted social services plan to do. Anyway, coffee? A man could die of thirst in this bloody house!'

I laughed again. We both knew the opposite was true. But by the time I'd made and poured the coffee, the atmosphere had changed. It had to. Since he was here I decided

I should quickly fill him in on the new disclosures poor Ashton had made to me.

John shook his head once I'd finished. 'Well, we're going to have to act on this, aren't we?'

I nodded. 'I bloody hope so! Kids generally don't just invent this sort of stuff, do they?'

'No, of course not. Though from what you say, we might have a problem. If he refuses to talk again about it, then we're stuck, of course.'

This was familiar territory. It had been exactly what had happened with Olivia. No wonder wily paedophiles could so often could get away with it.

'Let's hope he will, then,' I said, glancing at the clock. It was now eleven. 'Let's hope we can help him to feel secure enough to get all this stuff out.'

But there was no time to discuss things further and the doorbell rang again then, and we were soon all around the dining table, the meeting under way.

The findings had been pretty much as expected. Following a full psychiatric evaluation both parents had been formally declared unfit, unable to cope with the demands of everyday life, let alone care for five dependent children. The children had now been placed, therefore, in the care of the local authority, to safeguard their future wellbeing. But there was more, and this did come as a bit of a shock. It had been decided to split the children up. Ashton would be placed with one family, Olivia with another; both specialist carers, hopefully, though not specialists like we were. They would seek long-term foster families who fostered exclusively, ones who had no other day jobs and who'd received extra training. It was deemed that with such a history of neglect and damage these children needed that much input to recover and to thrive.

'But why separate them?' I asked Anna. 'That'll be devastating for them.'

'Well, one reason is simple logistics. It will be easier to place them if we split them. We're not exactly overrun with carers willing to take on two such troubled kids. The other reason is that because of what we've seen – and what your notes suggest, too – we feel Ashton has some kind of hold over the little one; that she relies on him too much to lead and direct her. We feel she'll be better able to let go of her feelings and adapt if she's in a different place to him.'

'And what about the younger three?' John asked. 'And what about sibling contact for all five of them?'

'Oh, they'll all have that, obviously, don't worry. I'm not sure how it's going to work yet, but we're going to make it twice yearly, at least, as a start point.'

Twice *yearly*? She was saying it as if it was actually twice *weekly*! I couldn't believe it. It just all felt so bleak. But John was speaking again. 'So have any potential placements been identified?'

Anna shook her head. 'Not yet. But you'll be pleased to know that my manager has now said that she's going to make a determined effort to find somewhere for them all ASAP.'

John's expression darkened. 'Well, no, Anna. That doesn't *please* me in the slightest. To be honest, I feel like we've been duped. What you say implies that she never had any intention of looking for a placement before now, which is the exact opposite of what we were told at the start of this process.' He stared hard at her. 'I'm not in the habit of making promises to my carers that I can't keep. I assured Casey and Mike that this placement with them would be for two to three weeks max. It's already been nearly four *months*. So what now?'

Anna reddened, and I couldn't help feeling a little sorry for her. But at the same time, I could see why John was angry. I'd never seen him so heated, and I knew he was only doing it out of genuine concern for my family. Anna quickly tried to justify her manager's intentions. 'I realise how it looks,' she said. 'But we have been trying, really. If we'd managed to find a suitable alternative before this, we would have, *of course*. And we do realise Mike and Casey don't normally do this kind of fostering –'

'Exactly!' John bristled. 'And which they can't currently do – having been trained at great expense in their speciality –'

'– and we really will be pulling out all the stops to get these kids placed.'

John got up then, with a terse-sounding 'Anyone need more coffee?', and I left him to fill the kettle while Anna – somewhat determinedly – steered the conversation back to what else had been said in court. Which soon diverted my attention from the OK Corral stand-off because there were new revelations, which were chilling.

Apparently 'Gwandad' had not only slept with the children's mother – his own daughter – he'd had relationships with *all* sorts of frighteningly young women. The whole file seemed to be full of similar allegations, most backed up by some pretty solid evidence. All that was lacking – and this was what threw me the most – was any evidence of anyone taking criminal action.

And there was more. I was also shocked to learn that the woman the kids called 'grandma' was no such thing. She was, in fact, the daughter of a neighbour! When his first wife had died, their grandad had started up a relationship with her, moved her in and immediately embarked on a relationship with her – as she was sixteen, there was nothing the parents could legally do. This relationship – it was unclear if they'd actually married – had then produced a further three children. It just got worse by the minute, and I couldn't help but shudder. The implications were almost too horrible to even contemplate. A choice not available to the offspring of this evil, evil man.

I was still reeling that night when I relayed everything to Mike. I'd wimped out of sitting down with the kids to spell things out. They hadn't asked and I'd decided that I'd wait until the next day. I wanted to be measured and in control when I told them, so I could support them, and right then, I didn't feel nearly calm enough.

'And I've been thinking,' I told Mike as I snuggled in bed beside him. 'We mustn't push this. Not now.'

'What do you mean?'

'I mean we mustn't put the pressure on for them to find somewhere. I don't want those little ones going *anywhere* till you and I are absolutely certain it's going to be perfect.'

'It'll never be perfect,' Mike said sadly. 'How can it, after everything?'

'I know, 'I said. 'But at least as perfect as can be.' I turned to face him. 'Deal? Because they really need us, don't they?'

Mike nodded. 'And now it's all out – now we know what we know, maybe the worst bit is over anyway.'

And perhaps he was right. We had to look forwards now, not backwards. From tomorrow we could start the lengthy process of re-building. Of the children grieving for their mummy, of course. That process had to happen. But, in a sense, maybe the worst for them *was* over now.

But not for me. I still had my worst bit to come. Tomorrow I had to tell them they were never going to see home again.

Just as well I was getting used to all this not sleeping malarkey.

Chapter 12

I had decided, during one of many bouts of sleeplessness that night, that the best time to tell the kids they wouldn't be going home again would be the evening, after tea, when Mike and Kieron would be there. It felt important that we showed a supportive united front. I also thought it would be better to do it at a time when their Ritalin would be wearing off, so that they'd be better able to digest what we had to tell them.

I felt certain Olivia would be hugely distressed; not only about her mummy, but also about her precious 'gwandad' – he was definitely the person that she talked about the most. Ashton's reaction, however, I really couldn't call. On the one hand he was fiercely protective of his mother, but on the other … this was a child who calmly sat down and asked me if he could stay and live with me and Mike for ever. I wished I could see inside his mind and get a sense of what was going on there. Just as with our first foster child,

Justin – around the same age when he'd come to us – I knew he'd seen too much, suffered too much, endured too much to bear, and I worried the damage would be irreparable.

We had pizzas for tea and after we'd finished Kieron suggested we all play Monopoly. Bless him, I thought, as I got the game out of the cupboard. He had this uncanny ability to know the right thing to do. A nice family board game would create exactly the right atmosphere in which to impart the grim news that had been hanging over me so much.

Our Monopoly set was a special edition one, with cartoon characters for pieces and all set in a theme park. The kids loved playing it, and I loved that they loved it, because it was a good way for them to improve their woeful maths, something I was keen to address. But we'd barely been playing for fifteen minutes before it had to be abandoned, when Olivia, sitting between Mike and I and waiting for her turn, asked,

'Casey? When will we see Mummy again?'

I glanced at Mike and Kieron, not sure how to answer. Now it had come to it, I couldn't seem to find the right words. I knew Ashton was now watching me intently. 'Um, well …' I began. 'We were going to talk to you both about that this evening. After our game, I thought, but …'

'Just *tell* us,' Ashton interrupted. 'We *know* it was all in court an' that.'

Mike cleared his throat. 'Quite so, Ashton. Tell you what, let's put the game on hold for ten minutes, shall we? And then we can tell you what we know.'

He hauled himself up – we were playing in a circle on the carpet, they way they liked to – and then picked up Olivia and popped her on the couch. 'C'mon, mate,' he told Ashton. 'Cuddle up. That's right.'

I remained kneeling on the carpet with Kieron, so I could talk to them at their level. My mouth was dry. 'Sweethearts, it's not good news, I'm afraid. The judge has decided that you need to stay in care. *All* of you. Your little brother and sisters as well. Which means ...' I paused, my eyes on Ashton, who was staring at me blankly. 'Well, it means you won't be able to live with Mummy anymore.'

'What, f'ever an' ever?' Olivia asked.

I nodded. 'At least till you're 18,' I said. 'Till you're grown-ups.'

She nodded slightly. 'So can we live with Gwandad instead?'

I shook my head. 'No, darling, that won't be possible, I'm afraid. The thing is' – oh, this was so hard – 'that you won't be able to see your family. Not for quite a long time now.' Even though it was me speaking the words, I could hardly believe I was hearing them. How did you explain something as enormous as that? And, moreover, how did you deal with being *told* it? The silence in the room was deafening. Why hadn't either of them reacted? I reached out and squeezed Olivia's hand. 'Which is very sad, I know, and I'm sure you're all *terribly* upset. But it's what the judge has said. Mummy and Daddy just aren't able to look after you, you see.'

I looked again at the pair of them, sitting there, evidently digesting it, and then Ashton did something that completely stunned me. He smiled. And then he shrugged. 'Okay then,' he said. 'We'll just stay here, then.'

He then turned to his sister. 'C'mon,' he said, jumping down and returning to his position on the carpet. 'I'm winning loads an' I wanna finish this game.' And Olivia, bright as a button, it seemed, duly followed him.

'My turn!' she said, reaching for the dice shaker from Mike.

We duly finished our game of Monopoly.

If I'd been stunned at the lack of reaction so, as the rest of the week went by, I felt it even more. I had been prepared for anything but this. Tantrums, tears, accusations, recriminations – since they'd been placed with us, these kids had been fiercely protective of and defensive about their family. And were it not for Ashton's admission to me about the abuse he'd suffered at the hands of his granddad, you could be forgiven for thinking their *own* perception of their tragic early upbringing was that it was perfectly normal. I couldn't even begin to work it out; couldn't make any sense of it at all, and as the week drew to a close, I felt no more enlightened. I was also concerned that Ashton obviously hadn't taken it in when I'd explained that they couldn't stay with us permanently. But perhaps that too was a coping mechanism. They were with us right now, weren't they? And with no-one suggesting any different, then perhaps that was good enough – enough for things around the house to return to normal.

Nothing in our house was normal these days, obviously – our norms these days being the constant battle against excrement being deposited in inappropriate places, the enduring shower-terror, the ADHD, the necessary vigil against unsavoury sexual goings-on – but, in terms of *our* normal, it was like any other week. In fact, measured against past weeks, it was a *good* week. The children were progressing well in so many ways, that it was as if they'd just blanked the whole idea that they'd ever had a family. It was as bizarre a situation as I'd ever seen. So all I could do was roll with it and await further developments, which I knew would be on the cards at some point.

And they were. The following Monday, I received a call from Anna, in what seemed like her never-ending quest to rattle my world.

'Casey,' she said, without preamble. 'Straight to the point. I've been consulting with John Fulshaw and a police liaison officer about the recent disclosures Ashton made to you.'

Ah, I thought. Progress. 'Good,' I said. 'I was wondering what was being done about that.'

'Well, quite a lot actually,' she said. 'And we need some help from you. We need you to go back and have a trawl through your records and write me a report concentrating on all the sexual stuff. You know, all the sexual references the children have made since they came to you. Ashton's recent one, obviously, but everything else too. Inappropriate touching, adult-type comments and so on.'

'I can certainly do that, no probs. Who do I send it to?'

'Email it to both John and I – and as soon as possible, if that's okay, because I want to come up Thursday, if that's going to work for you, to bring a police woman to interview them both.'

'A police woman? You know that'll scare them half to death, don't you?'

'She'll be in plain clothes, don't worry. Oh, and she'll need to speak to them separately. And I have to tell you, though you can sit in, you mustn't speak for them in any way. I'm afraid you really do just have to sit and listen. Even if it gets difficult ...'

'I understand that,' I said, feeling a little narked at being patronised. 'But don't get your hopes up. I very much doubt if the kids will talk. In fact, I'm sure they won't.'

'Quite possibly,' she conceded. 'But at least people are listening. Which is a start. We'll just have to see what happens, won't we?'

'I guess so. Oh, but one thing – should I tell the kids about this?'

'I'll leave that up to you. If you think it will help, then go ahead.'

'Mind you,' I said, thinking aloud now. 'There's Ashton. If he knows in advance, he'll have time to prime Olivia. Maybe I won't tell him anything.'

Mike agreed. When I put it to him that evening, he felt keeping schtum was the best plan. As he pointed out, Ashton was like a parent figure to his little sister. Which wasn't surprising. Being the oldest, and in the absence of proper parenting by any adults, she – and no doubt his younger siblings when they were still all together – naturally took her cues from him. And from what we'd witnessed since they'd been with us, my hunch was that he'd looked after his siblings, too. Making sure they got food, dealing with their problems, tending to them and comforting them if they were unhappy or grazed a knee. I felt a pang of sadness that, in all probability he'd be parted from them; go from much-loved big brother – which I didn't doubt he was – to having no-one. It all seemed so *bloody* unfair. What had any of them done to deserve the cards life had so cruelly dealt them? Nothing. And it made me so angry.

As it was half-term, the week was turning out to be a busy one. I'd spent a good deal of time taking the kids out to places, to the park, to go swimming and so on, mostly accompanied by Riley and Levi, but when Thursday came around I decided we'd stay in. I didn't want them over-excited or over-tired when the police woman came to see them, so I decided, since Halloween was fast approaching, that we'd have a day of baking, and got out my cake-making ingredients and my vast stock of food colourings. I had lots to use up because for our last foster child, Sophia, we'd put on a party based on the West End show *Wicked!*, so had just about every lurid colour imaginable.

We set about making a big batch of fairy cakes, which I told Olivia we could decorate with spiders and bats, and cookies in the shape of witches' hats.

'I am SO excited about Halloween!' she told me, as she carefully stirred the cake mix. 'Cos you know, Casey, at

Halloween all the mens and ladies give you moneys to give your mummy.' She turned to me. 'But you could have it this time,' she finished brightly. Though not shocked, I felt saddened at the picture she had painted. Of these kids going out – being sent out most probably – trick or treating, and having to hand over the spoils to the greedy adults – modern-day Fagins! – who waited at home while they worked.

But at least they were free of all that now, I reminded myself. And could be children – proper children – once again.

The baking, as it usually does when children are involved, took far longer and made far more mess than was comfortable for me to live with, so by the time we'd cooked and cooled, cleared and washed up it was almost three. Anna would be here with her police woman any minute. Mindful of her need to interview each child privately, I decided to set a station up at the dining table for the children. That way, while one was being interviewed in the living room, the other would be occupied in the dining room.

The two women arrived punctually and declined my offer of a drink; they seemed keen to get straight down to business. And with Ashton first, which made sense, since he was the oldest, and also the one who'd made the direct allegation. And right away I could tell that the mission would be fruitless. As I explained who the woman was and that she wanted to have a chat to him, everything about his body language made that abundantly clear.

'Hi,' she said warmly, offering a hand for him to shake. He didn't. 'My name's Lizzie and I'm a police lady and you must be Ashton. My word, you look very grown up for a 10-year-old!' He stood and scowled at her. 'And I'm here to chat to you,' she continued, 'about the things you told Casey about your granddad and your cousin.' She smiled encouragingly at him. 'Is that okay?'

Ashton remained mute and refused to sit down. I went and sat with Anna, in the corner.

'So,' Lizzie went on, 'd'you think you could tell me what you said?'

Now in his line of sight, Ashton transferred his scowl to me.

'C'mon, love,' I said. 'Why don't you sit down by Lizzie?' But he was having none of it. He folded his arms pointedly across his chest.

Lizzie tried another tack. 'Ashton,' she asked. 'Tell me, d'you know what sex is?'

Ashton slowly shook his head, looking straight at her.

'Okay,' she went on, 'tell me then, do you know what it means to touch someone where you shouldn't?' Once again, a slow, deliberate shake of the head.

'Alright,' she continued, 'Ashton, can you tell me if anyone's ever touched you on your privates?' The response was exactly the same. This went on through a good half-dozen further questions, till it seemed clear to everyone that Ashton was determined not to talk.

And it looked like being a repeat performance from Olivia initially. Naturally wary of the strange woman, she immediately clammed up. But it wasn't long before her natural chattiness returned, which made me wonder if her only reason for not doing so initially was because she'd been groomed to expect trouble if she spoke up.

But with very little prompting, she seemed to remember those days were gone now and that, in Casey's world, talking about things was good. Very soon in fact, she began to look as if she was having great fun. Yes, she knew what sex was, yes, people had touched her privates, yes to every question the stunned policewoman answered, accompanied by much girlish giggling.

'Do you want to tell me about it?' Lizzie asked her in response to these affirmations.

She nodded. 'Shall I come sit on your knee, like it's Santa?'

'Well, you could certainly come and sit *next* to me, if you'd like to. That way I can better see your pretty face.'

'You really a copper?' Olivia asked, once she'd settled herself beside her. 'You don't got no numiform on.'

'Ah,' Lizzie said. 'I see you're clever as well as pretty. So,' she said, 'can you explain what you mean when you say touching? And who was it touched your privates, Olivia?'

'Daddy did once,' she exclaimed proudly. 'He hurt my tuppence – you know, my pee pee? But he never meaned to. He said sowwy. He said sowwy, it was an accident. Cuz I was his bestest girl,' she finished brightly.

'How exactly did he hurt you, lovey?' asked Lizzie. 'In what way?'

Olivia smiled, then waggled a finger at the WPC, then laughed. 'Tut tut!' she said. 'Naughty! Don't you know that walls have ears?'

'That's a funny saying, Olivia. What does that mean? Can you tell me?'

Olivia shrugged. ''s what Ashton says. He says Mummy and Daddy say we mustn' tell tales an' if we did we'd get found out. Because walls have *ears*. An' they tell on you,' she finished.

Lizzie shook her head. 'Olivia, you know, that's just silly talk, sweetheart. Walls can't hear you. They're just bricks. And bricks can't talk, can they?'

Olivia shrugged again. 'Anyways, it don't matter. Cos we're not gonna see Mummy no more anyway, are we?' She then paused and seemed to think. 'But jus' cos you're a copper, don't you go blabbing to my brother. Or else he'll go an' give me a good hiding!'

Lizzie assured Olivia that she wouldn't and this seemed to make her happy.

'Can I go now?' she said. Lizzie told her that she could.

I took her back to her brother and she jumped up at the table, and was soon elbow deep in a gooey sticky mess. Ashton, still clearly upset, didn't even acknowledge her. I told the children I'd be back in a few minutes and returned to the living room.

'There,' I said to Anna. 'That's progress of a sort, isn't it? What Olivia's disclosed is surely enough to take things to the next stage, isn't it?'

Both women's expressions seemed to tell me I was wrong.

'Sadly,' Anna went on, 'it's not that simple. We've been here before, you see, with Olivia. It's all on file, from a couple of years back. She was taken to the doctor's with an injury between her legs. The father told the GP she had run into the corner of a coffee table, and the redness and bruising was perfectly consistent with that. Which means that if we offer this as evidence, he'll just refer straight back to that incident. It's not enough.'

'Not even with all the other things she said?'

'There's really nothing concrete enough. Nothing that could really be used in evidence.'

I was gobsmacked. 'What the hell does it take, then? Actually catching them in the act?'

'Trust me,' said Anna, 'I'm as angry as you are. Like you, my gut instinct is that there is just so much more to uncover here. But all we can do is keep trying to build our case. Watch and wait. Hope that one day, one of the kids will come up with something we can use, and, crucially, be prepared to repeat it. Honestly, Casey, that family will have their day in court, I promise.'

She turned then to the WPC. 'You know, I think it would be okay to tell Casey about the recent development, don't you?'

The WPC nodded. 'What development?' I asked.

'With the father. You didn't know this, but two days before the hearing, he was arrested. He's out on bail now, pending further enquiries – including this one – but apparently, when another female cousin heard about the case, and the fact that there was a slim chance they would have the children returned to them, she went to the police and filed a report accusing him of sexual abuse as well. On *her*, for many years, all through her childhood, apparently. Same as the one you already know about ...'

'So why wasn't this –' I started.

'We couldn't use it, Casey. His solicitor would have jumped on us for jeopardising his case. He'd been found guilty of nothing, at that point, remember. This has to be a whole separate process now.'

God, I thought. No wonder these kids exhibited so many signs of having been groomed. Granddad, the father – unrelated but both at it. Who else? Just how big a seam of evil ran through this family?

Chapter 13

It took Ashton some time to act normally around us again. I had all but given up on hoping he might revisit some of the things he'd told me in Wales, but I was concerned that the tentative trust had been broken – particularly after the police visit – and I was anxious to try and build bridges and to try and repair the damage before it all got too late.

Mike and I both went all-out to restore our relationships with him, making a point of spending more time with him individually, which did seem to help us make progress. Mike took him to work with him one day and allowed him to have a go driving a forklift truck, which he loved, and I made a point of arranging regular him and me time, taking him to the pictures to see a film he was particularly keen on, and reminding him that now, since he was that bit older than his sister, we could start to do things like that more often.

Two things were constantly on my mind. One was how important it was that we re-forged these bonds; if he was to be separated from all his siblings, his relationship with us would really matter, because having to venture into the unknown and live again (and alone) among strangers, meant it was vital that he knew we were all there for him.

The second was to continue to question that separation. Surely, despite the obvious logistical difficulties, it would be better to try and keep these two children together, at least? I understood what Anna had said about Ashton's controlling influence, but lots of kids – particularly in cases of poor, erratic parenting – looked up to older siblings in that way. Would it really be better for them all to be denied that bond? I wasn't convinced, and neither was Mike. We resolved to speak to John and Anna about it again.

For the moment, however, things were looking more positive. As Ashton began to relax, so the atmosphere improved, and by the beginning of November it felt – at least superficially – that we were back on a fairly even keel with them both. Indeed, there was an air of mild excitement in the house, because we'd told the children we'd take them to an organised Bonfire Night and firework display. Once again, we'd been shocked when Ashton revealed to us that they'd never done anything like that in their lives. If it had seemed incredible that they'd never so much as paddled in the sea, that they hadn't even done this took my breath away.

But they hadn't. All they'd done was to spot the odd firework in the distance, looking patiently out of a bedroom window. Most normal life, it seemed, had simply passed them by. It was heartbreaking to think about, it really was.

But my confidence about how much they'd all enjoy the action close-up was misplaced. We were only at the display – which had been put on by the local Rotary Club – for half an hour before we had to take them all home again. Olivia was simply petrified – both by the bangs of the fireworks *and* the bonfire – and though our first plan was for me to take her home while Mike stayed on Ashton, he was no more keen to stay at the display than his sister, so in the end we all trooped home together.

'It's because of the car being blown up,' Ashton explained to me. Mike was carrying Olivia, who was still terrified of all the noise, as we tramped the few streets back to home.

'Your car?' I asked.

He nodded. 'Yes, it was torched outside our house one day. Livs was only little and it really scared her, didn't it, Livs?'

Olivia merely whimpered, and burrowed her head into Mike's scarf.

Then she pulled her head back again and spoke. 'It was the bad mens!' she said. 'They didn' like our daddy, so they burned it!'

I wanted to dig further but I knew it needed to be very gently. 'Oh dear,' I said. 'Why'd they want to do such a thing, d'you think?'

'We don't know,' Ashton said. 'But they were definitely the same ones who wrote the bad stuff on our front door.'

'What bad stuff?' Mike asked.

'Kev the perv,' he said. 'Swear words.'

'That's not very nice.'

'No it wasn't,' Ashton answered. 'And when they done it, we kept getting picked on, too – at school.'

'That must have been hard,' I said. 'Was anything done about it? Did the police come?'

Ashton shook his head. 'Nah.'

'They tooked the car away,' Olivia said. 'Didn' they, Ash? Cos it was broken. They put it on this lorry and they tooked it away. We never had a car no more, after.'

Kev the perv, I thought. The family were clearly well known around the neighbourhood. Once again it seemed incredible that they'd hung on to the kids so long. And once again, I got the sense that there was so much more to know. I really felt we were just scratching the surface.

But for our own family, at least, it was a time of happiness. Riley was six months' pregnant now, so our next grandchild would soon be with us, a thought that, whenever I found myself bogged down in worries, would always bring a smile back to my face. Riley and David knew by now that they were going to have another boy, and they announced that they were going to call him Jackson. The kids seemed genuinely excited to share in this news, and even more so when Riley told them she was going to throw a party to celebrate Levi's second birthday. They positively beamed when she also told them that, because they'd been so good lately, they would have the special honour of being her official party helpers, choosing party food and helping with the decorating. They couldn't have been more excited about it all, and I sensed that we had really turned a corner.

But my bubble of happiness was destined to be popped. It was a couple of days before the party, and a regular Sunday evening. Because the children were both still frightened of the shower, and because their hygiene, even now, was somewhat haphazard, Mike and I still had to oversee bath-times. We'd got a routine now. Mike would invariably keep an eye on Ashton, while I would take charge of Olivia.

This particular Sunday, however, Mike was busy giving his car a bit of a valet; he'd washed it earlier and now wanted to give it a polish, so had relocated it back into the warmth of the garage so he could do it in the warm. Knowing how much time he could spend out there, if left alone with it, I decided to get on and bathe the kids without him. I did Ashton first, though, because he was keen to go back down and help Mike, as he'd been promised he could use the mini-vacuum.

Next up was Olivia, plus her favourite baby doll Polly, who'd been patiently waiting for her turn.

'Come on, sweetie,' I said, peeling off her sweater and joggers, while she busied herself removing Polly's babygro. She laughed as she usually did as I swung her into the bath-tub, but I noticed her wince as I sat her in the water.

'Oh, love, is it too hot?' I asked, dipping my arm in to check. Though I knew, because I'd already checked, it wouldn't be hot – only warm. She shook her head to confirm this, yet still she winced. 'A graze, then? A cut?' I asked.

Now she nodded. 'It was Ashton.'

'Ashton?' I asked her, not sure I'd heard right. 'What d'you mean?'

Olivia looked up at me, then turned her doll over and pointed. 'He been bummin' me,' she said, with a world-weary air.

It took a moment for what she said to properly sink in. Yet still it didn't. Did I really hear *that* right?

'Been *bumming* you?' I repeated.

She nodded. 'Yes. An it hurts a bit now it's in the water.'

I knelt beside the bath. 'Olivia, can you explain what you mean?' I asked her gently.

'You *know*,' she said. 'Lied on me. Like wot the growd-ups do. And hurt my bum.'

The picture she described to me felt all too believable. I'd seen them play-act a version of such things myself. But fully *clothed*, not naked. But from what she was saying ... I wasn't stupid. I knew these kids, left unsupervised, would fiddle with each other's genitals. But this – if true – was a whole different board game. Ashton was growing up. He'd be eleven soon. Starting puberty. And if he was already forcing himself on Olivia ... It didn't bear thinking about. I needed to act on this. Now.

I passed Olivia a flannel and suggested she wash Polly. 'I'll just be a minute,' I said, rising to my feet again. 'Got to go and have a quick word with Mike about something. Be back in no time, okay?'

I hurried downstairs and into the garage, where Mike was. Ashton was in the driver's seat of the car now, busy polishing the dashboard.

'Ash?' I said. 'Could you pop into the kitchen for a minute, love? There's something I need to talk to you about, okay?'

Ashton obediently did as I asked him, and when he'd gone back in I told Mike what Olivia had said. 'So maybe you could go up and wash her hair for her,' I suggested, 'while I deal with Ashton? I really need to speak to him about this.'

Mike shook his head as he wrung out his chamois. 'Lord,' he said, frowning, 'here we go again ...'

Back inside, I crossed the hall and entered the kitchen. God, I thought. Where do I even *start*?'

It might have been my imagination playing tricks on me, but as soon as our eyes met, I thought I could sense guilt. Which told me one positive thing at least, I thought, as I sat down with Ashton. If he *did* know what was coming and *was* feeling guilty, then that was progress. Easy to forget that a few short months ago none of these kids even knew sexual touching between them was wrong. Not that it made this any less unpalatable.

Ashton lowered his eyes as I sat down with him at the kitchen table. 'Ash, love,' I said, deciding to come straight to the point. 'What have you done to your sister? She says she's hurting.'

His eyes met mine again. 'I ain't done nothing,' he said quietly. 'Nothing at all. She's a liar.'

I kept my own voice low and level, to match his. 'Olivia is just a little girl, Ashton. Why d'you think she would lie about something like that?'

'I dunno,' he said. 'But she *is* lying. I done nothing.'

'Ashton,' I continued, 'I need you to tell me the truth. We will have to take Olivia to see a doctor, you see, so he can look at her bottom – which is where she says she's hurting. And we will have to tell the doctor what happened to cause it, and what Olivia has told me is that *you* hurt her bottom.' I held his gaze. 'Playing sex games. Is that true?'

'Not sex,' he said, shaking his head. 'It wasn't sex. She's a liar, saying sex. I didn't hurt her nowhere!'

Ashton put his head in his hands then, and refused to speak further, and I knew it would be pointless trying to make him. This shut-down, this closing off seemed very much a learned behaviour. Had they been taught that if they ignored something it would simply melt away? Well, this wouldn't. This couldn't. I needed to take this further. However grim a prospect it might be, and however it harmed our fragile relationship, I would be failing in my duty if I *didn't* take this further.

I'd heard Mike bringing Olivia back downstairs now, so I explained to Ashton that he had to go sit in the living room, as I had to go and phone the doctor. I made it clear I wasn't happy about whatever he had done. 'So why don't you think hard,' I told him quietly, as I ushered him out of the kitchen, 'about telling me the truth about this, Ashton?' Still not looking at me, he went into the living room. If he understood the implications of what I'd told him would now happen, he didn't show any outward signs that he was bothered.

Ashton dealt with, I then went into the hall and called EDT. EDT stood for the Emergency Duty Team – a team of mainly social workers, who were the first point of contact if anything happened to a child in our care out of hours. This was in order to get advice on what to do, obviously, but also to ensure that any incidents were reported and logged.

In this case the on-duty social worker advised me that I should call the local hospital right away. She told me that I should ask to be put through to the duty paediatrician and to explain that Olivia was a looked-after child, together with the nature of the incident and alleged injury. This was to ensure, I was told, they'd act promptly.

I was shocked but pleased that she'd been right; it was quick. Within minutes we were talking to the on-call paediatrician, who told Mike and I to bring Olivia around to the hospital right away. I was keen to have Mike along, as I felt sure that what was going to happen, examination-wise, would probably distress Olivia (who was probably used to her brother's 'attentions') a whole lot more than the original incident.

Riley, bless her, stepped in, and was around at ours in minutes, so within the hour we were clustered, beneath the bright lights of the A&E department, while the paediatrician examined a very agitated Olivia.

As I'd expected, she was terribly traumatised. And I was hardly less so, as I fought against her writhing so that the doctor could examine the area properly.

'Stop it!' she was sobbing. 'Stop the bad man, please, Casey! I don't want my bum touched! Go away!'

Thankfully, the paediatrician decided that, in this case, he wouldn't need to do anything internal. 'There don't seem to be any signs of actual penetration,' he reassured us. 'What I suspect we might have had here is just an act of simulation, which might have caused some bruising and soreness. But that's all, in my opinion. You say the brother's 10?'

We confirmed that he was – just – over the cacophony of Olivia's protests, and the doctor confirmed that that would be in keeping with what he'd seen; that it would be unusual and unlikely that a boy of that age would be physically able to do any more than that. 'Though I'll obviously liaise with social services where required,' the doctor finished. 'And well done you,' he said warmly, to a very shaky Olivia. 'Here –' he reached across us to a small plastic pot in a side shelf. 'Here's a sticker for being *such* a brave girl.'

It was mid-evening by the time we left the hospital, bitingly cold and dark now, and it occurred to me again that for Olivia – still clinging to me like a limpet, still trembling and tearful – *this* would be the bad part, the traumatising memory. Not Ashton 'bumming' her: that might have hurt, but who knew? The grim truth was that it might be all par for the course for her, whereas, sticker or no sticker, the prodding and poking by a scary stranger in a white coat was clearly a very frightening experience.

We stopped at McDonald's on the way home, to get her an ice-cream, to cheer her up. We must have looked a sorry sight, the three of us, huddled around out little table. Two fraught-looking parents, and a tot in her pyjamas, even if she did brighten somewhat. And, even so, it was still the proverbial Band-Aid on a big, gaping wound. Dare we even now let the two of them out of our sight?

No. What a mess. What a horrible, ugly mess. And not a single sign of light on the horizon.

Chapter 14

I didn't have a clue how to turn things around with Ashton. He seemed to hate us now. Why wouldn't he? Didn't matter how much we told him the thing he'd done was wrong, unless he understood that himself it would essentially just cast us in the role of horrible foster carers, intent on making his life even more of a misery than it already was.

I kept going back to what he'd told me about what his grandfather had done to him, and how he'd been made to do the same to his little cousin. Should I really have been shocked that he'd tried to do the same to Olivia? Perhaps not, but it was still a measure of how much his life experience had warped his mind that he was clearly unhappy at the sexual abuse that had been done to him, distressed about the things he'd been made to do to his little cousin, but at the same time thought nothing of trying to do that very thing with his own sister. This was why sexual abuse of the young was such a canker. Prior to their own sexual awakening they would soak it up as 'normal' every bit as readily as they would the art of using cutlery. And he was *ten*. So while there might be a good chance for his younger siblings, time – time in which to re-programme that troubled mind of his – was a commodity in very short supply.

The day after the hospital visit Ashton didn't speak to me at all. If I spoke to him, he snarled, and otherwise, he ignored me. It was obvious I wasn't going to be able to break through to him any time soon. Olivia, on the other hand, seemed fine. By the following morning, the trauma of the hospital done with, she was back to her usual happy self. And, bar the sore bottom, why would she be concerned about what had happened? It was becoming depressingly clear that it had probably been happening – or some version of it anyway – for much of her tragic young life.

But for me, it was just all so depressing. And not just me, either, Kieron too. I'd filled him in the previous day and his expression had said it all. But it felt wrong to hide this sort of stuff from him. The day I kept secrets from my nearest and dearest would be the day I must hang up my fostering hat. Predictably, of course, he was distraught. But then, perhaps he should be. This was the reality we were living through. No point in sugaring the pill about kids like these two, and if Kieron was serious about wanting to work with damaged and dispossessed youngsters, he needed to go in with his eyes open.

'You know, Mum,' he said now, 'I just keep going over and over it. How *could* he?'

Kieron had just returned from Lauren's, where he'd stayed over, as he often did now, and was keen to hear if anything had been done.

'I know,' I said, shaking my head sadly.

'So what will happen?'

'I don't know yet. I've still got to speak to John and Anna.'

'It's bad, though, isn't it?'

'Yes, love. It's bad. We just have to work out what's the best way to deal with it. But I'm sure once I've spoken to John, we'll be able to form a plan.'

Kieron looked completely unconvinced as I said this. I hoped the reality didn't match his cynical expression. I hoped he could witness some sort of happy outcome for these little ones, particularly after the trauma of Sophia. That had been tough for him. Still continued to be, really. Though she was making good progress in the adolescent unit where she lived now, happy families might never be an outcome for her.

Kieron went up to his bedroom to get changed, and I went to make myself a cup of coffee. It was automatic with me; it was my miracle cure for everything. Where others administered sweet tea for shock, I dosed myself up on coffee when down.

Coffee and a cigarette, ideally, and even though it was perishing, I dutifully took both into the garden. I'd always smoked in the conservatory – the one place the rest of the family allowed it – but since the little ones had come, I'd stopped. It just didn't seem right. But now winter was setting in with a vengeance, I reflected, shivering, I might just have to come good on the promise I'd made Mike to quit as soon as it got too cold to smoke outside.

But today wasn't that cold. Or at least, that was what I told myself. I'd just have this cigarette and call John.

But Anna beat me to it. I came inside to hear the phone already ringing.

'I just read your email,' she told me. 'And saw the EDT report flagged up, too. How are you? How is everything there now?'

'Well,' I said. 'Ashton's not speaking – he's very angry, I can tell. Olivia's fine, though. It's like she's forgotten all about it.'

'And did the hospital say they intended to follow things up?'

'I don't think so. I think they're just going to notify social services.' Another report in another file, to be stashed in a drawer.

'They're not involving the police, then?'

'Not as far as I know. Are they meant to?'

Only if they believe an actual abuse took place. But from what you said in your email, it sounds to me like they must have decided to just put it down as horseplay.'

'I bloody hope not!' I said. How could this all be normalised so readily? To my mind the only reason for there being no penetration was that with Ashton being so young, it wasn't physically possible. But it soon would be. It was what was in his *head* that mattered, surely?

'Look,' I said, 'I know it wasn't actually that, but still. It *could* have been. That certainly seemed to be the intention. He needs help, Anna. Counselling ... to stop this rot before it –'

'I know,' she interrupted. 'And it's awful. Really awful. We need to put more strategies in place for you, Casey. I know you're sort of out on a limb over there, and we need to give you more in the way of help. I've already spoken to John Fulshaw this morning and if it's alright with you, we'll both come to visit you next Wednesday, and see what we can come up with between us.'

More talk, I thought irritably, as I agreed to her arrangements. *It's action I want, not bloody words!*

Though when I spoke to John afterwards, it was as if he'd read my mind. He told me he'd handed social services an ultimatum. He said he'd demanded that if I didn't get extra help, then they would have to look for an alternative interim placement. Which wasn't what I wanted at all. I knew he was trying to be helpful, but I didn't want these kids wrenched away from us. I wanted to see this thing through. I wanted to be sure that, when they did finally leave us, that would be it. No more moves. A permanent placement; not have them shunted all over the place. Yes, it did mean our lives would continue to be chaotic, but, as I so often reminded myself, this was exactly what Mike and I had signed up to do.

* * *

But Kieron hadn't, and it was to be only a couple of days later that this hit home very hard. It was Friday evening and Kieron had brought Lauren over, and once the children were in bed, and we were about to settle down and watch some telly, they asked if they could both have a word with us.

My first thought – not surprisingly – was the obvious one. I didn't mean to, but found myself looking straight at Lauren's stomach, thinking uh, oh, I think I know what's coming. To be fair to myself, this wasn't completely unwarranted; Riley and David had done almost exactly the same thing when they broke the news that they were going to have Levi.

Kieron must have noticed my panicked expression, because he immediately laughed out loud. 'Mother, it's not that!' he said, guffawing. 'Don't be daft! Lauren's not pregnant!' At this I could see Mike grinning too. 'God!' Kieron went on. 'You must be mad if you think that! We're far, far too young and irresponsible for that!'

Lauren went scarlet. 'Casey!' she admonished. 'I'm not daft!'

'I never said a word!' I blustered back at them. 'I didn't think any such thing, as it happens!' And I remembered to thank God, as I said it, too. Much as I loved babies, I would have been worried if Lauren had been pregnant right now. Kieron got stressed out enough by life as it was. He wasn't ready. Not one bit. We all knew that.

'Anyway,' he went on, he face becoming more serious. 'Me and Lauren have been thinking about this ... thinking for a while now. The thing is that Lauren's mum and dad have got a massive house – miles too big for just the two of them, and, well, they've offered us the top floor. There's a little kitchen, and a bathroom, and all we have to do is pay them a small …'

He tailed off, obviously seeing my face fall.

'But why? Why d'you want to leave?' asked Mike. Then he checked himself. 'Sorry. I should rephrase that. I know you two …' He smiled at them both now. 'I know you're close. But why now, particularly? It's not because how things have been at home lately, is it?'

I was glad he was speaking for me. All sorts of things were going through my head.

'It's not that, Dad,' Kieron was saying. 'It's just sensible. I'm 20 now. Old enough to be standing on my own feet. And Lauren's mum said she'll save half of whatever we pay in rent – put it in an account for us so that when the time feels right, when we're ready to go and live on our own, we'll have money saved up for a deposit.'

Which all made sense. 'Oh, but Kieron,' I said. 'Are you sure you're not doing this because of the kids? Because if that's the case, you know there is honestly no need. They won't even be here for that much longer, and –'

'Casey, it's not that, really,' said Lauren firmly. 'We've been thinking about it for a long time.'

'We *want* to do it, Mum,' Kieron added gently. 'I spend most nights there anyway. It's only fair that I start paying rent to Lauren's parents.' He smiled at me. 'And, Mum, d'you really want me to be that kid who spends the rest of his life with his parents and never leaves home?'

Sad as it was, I knew I could only agree with them. It did make sense. It was a good way for Kieron to experience independence, but with a safety net. At least I wouldn't have to worry about him struggling in some crappy flat and feeling too proud to ask for help.

'Well, if that's what you both want,' I said. 'Then of course it's the right thing to do. You know where we are ...' I let the sentence go unfinished. Kieron knew what I meant. He knew he had more challenges to face than most. But it didn't need spelling out. This was a positive development. That empty nest was always coming, and I just had to face it. I kept the smile firmly glued to my face.

It was tough, though. That weekend, Kieron, Mike and Lauren's dad moved all of Kieron's things down to Lauren's, and it hurt. And after cleaning his room – important to keep super-busy, I decided – I set about transferring all Ashton's things into it, so that I wouldn't have to look at it empty and son-less for so much as a minute longer than I had to. The room Ashton had been in could go back to being spare. So much better than seeing Kieron's empty.

'You'll enjoy being in here,' I told Ashton brightly, as we brought in the last of his DVDs and toys. 'Lots more space,' I said, 'and look! You can see the park from the window in here!'

Eventually, I could see a flicker of interest. He was trying hard, still, not to engage positively with me, but the barriers were coming down, bit by tiny bit.

'Casey,' he asked, 'would I be allowed a CD player? You know, for my room, so I could listen to music?'

'Of course, love,' I said. 'That's a brilliant idea. Tell you what, when I go to the supermarket later, I'll get you one. Might even stretch to some new CDs, too. What's that stuff you like? That silly rapping stuff? Some with that on?'

The face he pulled was priceless, and it cheered me up no end, because it was like watching Kieron all over again. 'God, Casey, don't you know *anything* about music? It's not rap, it's hip-hop. Like my mum used to like.' He grinned, and it looked genuine, and I felt all the better for it. It was the first smile I'd got out of him in days.

And as the rest of the afternoon wore on, I began to see more positives. The move would be good for Kieron – I could see that more and more now – and at the same time, it would make my life just that little bit less stressful, now that I wouldn't fret about my sensitive son having the reality of such troubled kids rammed daily down his throat.

No, that was our job. We'd planned on homemade chicken curry and egg fried rice for our tea, which Mike had volunteered to make, bless him. But, as Mike was a bit of a stress head in the kitchen, I had sensibly decided not to volunteer to help. So after I'd done the shop and got the CD player and a new colouring book for Olivia, I forwent the chance to play *commis* chef in our kitchen, and instead volunteered to take charge of bathing Olivia. Mike had almost finished anyway, and had promised Ashton that as soon as the curry was in the oven, they could play on the PlayStation together; a treat which Ashton really loved.

'Polly needs a bath too, don't forget,' Olivia told me, as we went up to her bedroom and helped her get undressed. 'Babies get so dirty, don't they, when they've been out playing all day?'

I smiled at her quaint chit-chat – she really was a sweet endearing child – and agreed that, yes, Polly needed a bath too. Olivia's new favourite doll (not the raggedy one she'd arrived with, thank goodness, even if she did share her name) was practically a part of the family now. She accompanied us everywhere, had to be kissed goodnight at bedtime, and even had a place set up at the table at mealtimes if she happened to be downstairs when we ate.

'Okay, love, 'I said to her, as we weren't in any hurry. 'How about you bath Polly while I change your sheets, then I'll be back to help you wash your hair, okay?'

She smiled happily as I lifted her into the bathtub and passed her the now undressed doll.

I left her for ten minutes, stripped the bed and re-made it, before returning to shampoo her hair for her. But when I entered the first thing I saw were some wet footprints, where she'd obviously got out of the bath. She was back in it now, but the next thing I noticed was that she was now wearing a pair of clear plastic gloves that had come from a carton of my hair dye. The box was open by the sink. Hence the footprints. But it was what she was doing, gloved up, that really stunned me. Too absorbed to notice me, she was very busy, carefully inspecting between the doll's legs, and making a poking motion with her finger.

I moved closer to the bath and asked her what she was doing. She really jumped, then, and dropped the doll in fright.

'Oooh, you scareded me, Casey!' she said, patting her heart dramatically.

'I'm sorry, sweetheart, 'I said, 'I didn't mean to. Why the gloves?' I asked conversationally, as she retrieved the doll from the water. 'And what were you doing with Polly?'

'Oh, I'm just giving her an internal,' she answered, her fright over. 'Don't worry,' she said brightly. 'It doesn't hurt her.'

'An internal?' I said lightly. 'What's an "internal", sweetie?'

She smiled knowingly, and in that instant, a sudden thought occurred to me. That I probably shouldn't worry about becoming de-sensitised. What she was saying – and its implication – made me feel sick.

'Silly Casey,' Olivia said, shaking her head. 'Don't you know? You can get stuff stuck up there. You know. In your tuppence. That's why *all* liccle girls have to have internals.'

Chapter 15

I called Anna the next morning. I felt helpless; I hadn't even really known what to *say* to Olivia, let alone what to do. All I could do was what I *did* do; record it and report it. And as ever the advice was the same.

'Remain vigilant,' Anna told me. 'And keep recording everything, obviously. That's all you *can* do.'

Which wasn't much help. 'But you know what?' she suggested. 'Perhaps it would be a good idea if I came for a special visit and perhaps gave her a bit of a biology lesson using her dolly; see if we can find out a bit more about where her knowledge lies.'

I was conscious that Anna's motivation might be more about securing more evidence against the family than worrying about the urgent need for help for these kids. 'I could probably do that myself,' I answered shortly, 'rather than you having to drag up here.'

Her response, after a brief pause, was interesting. 'You know, Casey,' she said – had she read the irritability in my tone? – 'if this is all becoming a bit too much for you, we could try to find some respite care for the kids for a couple of days. Would that be helpful?'

Helpful? I politely declined her offer. *No*, I thought, that *really is not* what I need.

But Anna's comments did at least energise me. Over the next couple of days I trawled the internet to try and find some information about sex education, and what would be appropriate to discuss with children of different ages. I felt sure that Olivia was still too young to be told anything graphic, but these were not normal kids, and had been exposed to sexual practices, and I felt strongly that there must be something I could do to help. I simply couldn't just sit there and have Olivia do things like she had to her doll and just observe and record and report them. This child – *both* these children – needed these things addressed, and it needed to start happening as a matter of urgency. To just stand and watch – to not point out that the things they were doing were inappropriate was tantamount to actually reinforcing them. Every episode left unchallenged brought them closer to a point where they might be scarred irreparably, for life. Was there anyone who hadn't heard the familiar – and true – adage that abused children often went on to abuse?

But my investigations threw up something positive at least. I was out of touch, these days, with the various childhood ages and stages, so it was news to me that apparently Olivia *was* already at an age when she should know about reproduction, recognise and name body parts and be able to talk about feelings and relationships. That was all the encouragement I needed. I would give her that biology lesson myself.

I don't know what a casual observer might have thought had they happened upon Olivia and me in the kitchen a week later, with our two new temporary members of the family, Mr and Mrs Gingerbread, which I'd bought from the local supermarket, and accessorised myself – with a little bit of white writing icing in the places I wanted to discuss.

But though Olivia was giggling – I'd decided to leave Ashton out of this one; he was in the other room, on the PlayStation – I was in deadly earnest about this.

'Casey, you're so rude!' Olivia laughed, once I'd got her sitting up at the table and explained what we were going to talk about. 'Look! This one's got boobies and a tuppence!'

She giggled. 'An' this one got boobies and a pee pee! You can't have boobies *and* a pee pee, Casey!'

I was about to answer, when Olivia corrected herself. 'Actually, you can, can't you? Mens got boobies, but only tiny. Only the ladies got milk. That's right, innit, Casey?'

I nodded. 'Yes, that is right, Olivia,' I agreed. 'Only ladies have milk in their breasts. Do you know why that is?'

Olivia adopted her knowing expression. 'I'm not stupid!' she informed me. 'It's to feed their kids, of course!' Upon which, grinning impishly at me, she picked up Mr Gingerbread, and bit off his head.

This was beginning to feel a little pointless. 'My mummy's got fat boobies!' she then informed me, through her mouthful. 'Big old boobies. Like footballs!' she said, gesturing with her free hand. 'Gwandad always used to say that,' she added, by way of explanation. Mr Gingerbread, I could see, was now half the man he had been.

This *was* pointless. Perhaps I should leave it to Anna after all. 'Come on,' I said, picking up Mrs Gingerbread and snapping an arm off. 'How about you help me make tea then? Meatballs and spaghetti. Kieron and Lauren are coming.'

'Yeah!' she trilled, beaming happily at me, and looking for all the world like a bright-eyed little innocent who wouldn't yet know one single inappropriate thing about tuppences and pee pees or anything else. Such a wicked twist of fate that she was not.

It hadn't been as bad as I'd expected, Kieron moving out, because he'd been home almost as many times as there'd been days since he'd left. Indeed, on more than one occasion, he'd just turned up as usual, yelling 'I'm starving! What's for tea, Mum?' as he came in. So we made plenty of meatballs, and it was just as well we did, because Riley and David turned up for tea too. And it was an absolute joy to have the whole brood together. Not just for us, but for the little ones as well. And all the talk was about Levi's upcoming birthday.

It hardly seemed possible that my first grandchild was going to be two already. It seemed only yesterday that I'd watched him being born. But an awful lot had happened since he'd come into the world. It was no exaggeration to say our lives had changed dramatically. But all for the good, I thought, even if it had been challenging sometimes. We might have had our stressful moments, but on the whole, I felt happy and fulfilled.

And definitely up for a party. And, as per the Watson family tradition, Levi's wasn't going to be a low-key affair. Riley had already hired a local hotel for it; one that had established a reputation locally for providing brilliant birthday parties, themed to whatever was your choice.

Riley had refused to spill the beans on what she'd decided upon for Levi, but when the following Saturday came around, it was clear what it was as soon as we pulled up in the car park. We were greeted by staff wearing Teletubbies costumes and greeting us all pretty manically. Half of the car park was already cordoned off too, to house a giant bouncy castle, from which hung a banner that said 'Hip hip hooray! Levi's 2 today!'

'This is fantastic, love!' I said, as I took it all in. And it was. There was a wooden bridge, which led to the back door of the hotel, which was decked out with balloons and cardboard daisies. Even the ground was decorated – with big splats of red and yellow, which were presumably supposed to be jelly and custard – the Teletubbies' favourite.

'You wait till you get inside,' Riley told me excitedly. 'Honest, Mum, you ain't seen nothing yet!'

But the children, like all the other little guests, only had eyes for the bouncy castle, so, even though it was a bitterly cold November day, I was happy to stay outside and supervise for a bit. Not that I needed to do much. The hotel staff, all in costume, were doing a wonderful job, keeping Levi's playgroup friends, plus all his cousins, plus my two, entertained with lots of games and silly dances.

But eventually the weather drove most of us gratefully inside, and, despite a few clinging tenaciously to the small fence around the inflatable, the little ones' attention was soon readily diverted by the delights on offer in the warmth of the function room. Here too, they'd done Levi proud for his birthday. They'd created a setting just like the original, complete with cut-outs of daisies and other Teletubbies characters and, the *pièce de résistance*, at the far end of the room – an actual working jelly and custard machine, which looked just like the one on TV.

Ashton and Olivia were speechless, and looked around the room open-mouthed, eyes like saucers.

'Oh my gosh!' said Olivia in awe. 'Look at all this! Oh, where's Levi? I want to show him all the pretty flowers. He loves flowers!'

Touched, I pointed him out to her. 'I'll bet he'd love that,' I agreed. 'Go on, then. But remember, no picking him up, okay?'

I had to take care with Levi where Olivia was concerned because, being the second of five, she had no qualms about marching around holding little ones. It had probably been a big part of her young life. But she nodded obediently and trotted over to Riley, who I knew I could rely on to keep an eye on her.

I turned to Ashton. More self-conscious than his little sister, he seemed to be finding the whole thing just a little bit overwhelming. 'Go on,' I told him. Why don't you go and join in with your sister? Or maybe go and get some food from the buffet.'

Ashton still seemed reluctant to leave my side, perhaps shy about helping himself among all these strangers. 'You hungry?' I asked him. I nudged him. 'I'm surprised you weren't the first there!'

I was, too. Though we'd not seen the stark evidence of it that Olivia had displayed when she'd first come to us, Ashton cared about food and when it was coming. Not to the extent of our first foster child, Justin, who had to know exactly what the next meal would be, and when. But Ashton did worry about it and, like Olivia had that first night, he still sometimes binged on it and hid it. Where his little sister seemed to have settled down in that regard, he'd often still squirrel away biscuits in his room. These were understandable behaviours, given both the children's shocking background. But in the midst of all the sexual stuff going on with these kiddies, perhaps I'd not fully grasped the true extent of Ashton's obsession with the everyday business of getting fed.

'I'm starving,' he said now. 'But I can't go by myself. I don't know what to get.'

'Love, you can have anything you fancy. That's the point of a buffet. You get a plate and then you choose the things you like best.' His brow furrowed as I said this and he looked unconvinced. I took his hand. 'Tell you what, shall I come with you?'

He shook his head then, his pride clearly coming to the fore. 'I'm okay,' he said, wriggling his hand from my grasp. 'I'm fine.'

And, oh, how I wish I'd just gone with him.

As it was, I watched him walk across to the room to the groaning table, where at first it seemed nothing was amiss. He filled a plate with food, nibbling on a sandwich as he did so, and I was so busy chatting to one of Riley's friends about her children that it was a while before I realised he hadn't moved away. He seemed rooted to the spot, clutching his full plate of food, just looking from side to side at all the half-full platters, as if unable to tear himself away.

The next bit seemed to happen in slow motion. I saw David go over to him and then smile and say something, and, from what I could see, gently try to steer him away. Ashton's response was to put down his plate and then grip the buffet table with both hands. It was difficult to be clear about what happened next because there were children playing between us, which kept obscuring my sight-line, but when I saw David wincing and hopping on one leg, I hurried over to see what was going on.

'He stamped on my bloody foot!' he said. 'Hard!' He glared at Ashton, who was still clinging on to the edge of the table. 'Look, lad,' he said to him. 'You've had *enough* now!' He turned to me. 'He's not stopped, Casey. Been stuffing food down his throat now for close on twenty minutes. Honestly, he'll be sick if he carries on.'

'Ashton, come on, love,' I tried. 'You've had enough.'

'No!' he practically snarled at me. 'There's still loads here. I *can't!*'

Just then, a young mum approached the table with two little ones and reached out to take a couple of iced buns.

'Gerroff!' Ashton snapped at her. 'They're mine. Just leave off!'

'Ashton!' I barked. 'They are *not*! They're for everyone!'

His face was a mask of distress by this time, and before I could really register what had happened, he kicked out at the startled woman, his foot delivering what would have been a pretty painful blow had she not darted sideways to avoid it. And the same fate befell another child, who'd dared to approach. It was only my yanking Ashton smartly backwards that spared another unsuspecting shin from getting whacked.

People were looking towards us now, aware of the growing commotion. 'Get off!' he screamed. 'Tell them, Casey! Tell them! It's all gonna be gone!' He had tears in his eyes and was trembling with anger and it became clear that I was witnessing behaviour around food that was every bit as troubled as Justin's had been. He simply couldn't deal with seeing so much food in one place at one time without needing, not just wanting – compulsively needing – to eat or hide away every scrap. In short, he could not walk away from it. Years of chronic hunger had so damaged his psyche that his response was as powerful as it was instinctive. The only reason I'd yet to see it was because he'd not been in this situation. He couldn't help it, I realised. He had no control over it.

Smiling apologetically at the growing crowd, and anxious not to cause a scene that might spoil the party, I gently prised Ashton's white fingers from the edge of the table. Then, with David to help me, I forcibly, but calmly, led him from the room, trying to ignore the screams of protest and the wildly thrashing limbs, which were a distressing enough sight as it was, and meant the people closest had to hurriedly shimmy out of the way. Already a couple of the little ones had started crying and, as I passed him, I could see my little grandson was one of them, looking petrified at the sight of this hysterical, flailing boy.

It was a job to contain him, but we were eventually through the doorway, upon which, sensing our grip on him loosening, Ashton wriggled free of us both and threw himself on the floor.

'Go back in,' I told David. 'Get back to the party. I'll sort Ashton out.'

'You sure?' He looked sceptical.

'Absolutely,' I said. 'Just got himself into a bit of a state.'

David still didn't look convinced, and I did understand his reticence. I was five foot nothing, and Ashton wasn't much shorter. But he had no fight left in him, and was no threat to anyone. He just needed comforting, that was all.

Once David had gone back in, I sat down on the floor beside him, stroked his hair and tried my best to console him.

'It's okay,' I said softly. 'I understand, Ashton. That was hard for you, wasn't it? Seeing all that food and not being able to –'

'But you don't understand!' His face was running with tears now. 'You don't understand! It's your fault! I coulda had that! An' now it'll get wasted! And I'll starve! You're so cruel to me, Casey! You just want me to starve!'

'Don't be daft, love,' I said. 'Why on earth would I want to starve you? I feed you enough, don't I? I give you lots and lots of food. But you know what? I do understand how you feel, you know. How you must fret about going hungry. I get that, I really do.'

But Ashton was still too upset to be mollified. He was now a picture of perfect misery. And all over a few sandwiches and sausage rolls. I should have thought. I should have realised. I should have prepared him better. And because I hadn't, this had ruined Levi's party. 'I don't care,' he sobbed. 'I just wanna go home. They can keep it. They can throw it all away. I DON'T CARE!'

'Okay, love. That's okay,' I said, hugging him to me. He was now like a big floppy rag doll. 'We'll get you home, okay? And then you'll feel a whole lot better.'

I popped back inside and explained to Mike what was happening, knowing David would be happy to drop off him and Olivia. Then we slipped out the back and went home.

Chapter 16

'You know what?' Mike said to me the following evening, as the pair of us tackled the mound of Sunday dinner washing-up. 'I really think we have to *do* something about these kids, love. I mean, look at Ashton's behaviour. Remember Justin?'

I nodded as I passed him the roasting tin to dry. And laughed ruefully. 'How could I forget?'

'Exactly,' he said. 'And that was the first thing I thought about when he kicked off on Saturday. That this is not just ADHD. The poor kid has serious issues going on. Which nobody seems to be taking remotely bloody seriously!'

This wasn't strictly true. There *would* be help forthcoming eventually. But since CAMHS wouldn't get involved until the kids were placed permanently, the net result was the same as if the situation *wasn't* being taken seriously. Nothing was being done now, and nor would it be. Mike was right in what he said, and the party had been a catalyst. Every day that went by was another day wasted. So if no-one else was prepared to step in and do something, then perhaps I should do it myself.

I called Dr Shackleton first thing on the Monday and, as ever, he was incredibly helpful. He'd been our GP for years, since long before we started fostering, and now we were, he couldn't have been more supportive.

'So they're getting nothing in the way of counselling at present?' he wanted to know.

'Nothing,' I confirmed. 'They're just on medication for the ADHD, as you know, but they're all in such a mess, in one way or another – particularly Ashton – and getting a settled place, and so some support from CAMHS, might take months yet. And the longer this goes on, the worse I think they'll get. It just all feels so *wrong* to be doing nothing.'

'Leave it with me,' he said. 'I come up against this sort of thing all the time. Red tape's all well and good, eh? But sometimes it needs cutting. Let me see if I can get the ball rolling for you.'

I felt much better having spoken to Dr Shackleton. When he said he'd make things happen, he generally did. And I felt even better when I then called John Fulshaw and learned that he completely supported my decision. 'Mind you,' he said, 'brace yourself, because Anna won't like it. Protocols and all that. Proper CAMHS procedure. She'll be cross you didn't talk this all through with her first.'

'But if I did that she'd just tell me not to. You know that.'

'Yes I do, and between you and me, I agree with you. You and Mike are the ones at the front-line in all this. If they expect you to care for these children properly, it's faintly ridiculous not to give you a degree of autonomy. No, you did the right thing, Casey, and I'm one hundred per cent behind you. Let me know how it goes. Keep me posted.'

John turned out to be right. Anna was definitely sniffy. The next day, no less, I received a curt email informing me that while it was perfectly okay for me to organise routine doctor's appointments (which was kind of her) I must 'in future inform a member of the team before making decisions of this nature'.

Suitably chastised, though not in the least repentant, I composed an appropriately apologetic email in reply, ensuring her I had definitely taken all her advice on board, and would of course do as she asked 'in the future'. It was easy to press 'send', I thought, smiling, as I did so, because I'd already done what I'd set out to.

But I was soon to find out that the politics of the care system were more complex and frustrating than even *I* had thought. The following week, I took a call from Julia Styles, the special needs co-ordinator at the children's primary school. I knew Julia quite well because our paths had crossed for years. She'd recently transferred to the primary from our local secondary school, which was not only the school our first foster child, Justin, had attended, but was also the place where I'd worked for several years, before Mike and I had trained as foster carers.

'It's nothing to worry about,' she said, because of course that's what I'd done. I'd not long dropped the children and automatically assumed there had been some sort of problem with one of them.

'I'm glad to hear that,' I said, relieved.

She laughed. 'It's just admin, in the main. It's just that we've finally received the records from the children's old school, and it's left me with something of a conundrum, to be honest. Because they don't seem to bear any real relation to the reality of the kids themselves, you know?'

'You've only just got them?' I mentally calculated. 'But it's been almost four months!'

'They've certainly not hurried themselves, that's for sure,' she said. 'And now I've got them, I'm a little confused. Honestly, Casey, if you read them you'd hardly think they described the same children!'

'In what way?'

'Well, it's obviously not for me to make assumptions, but according to these records, the children, when transferred, seemed to be down as having no significant problems.'

'But we both know that's not true.'

'Exactly. In fact my recommendation, having now reviewed this first half-term, is that they both have some degree of learning disability, so they should be spending time in our learning support unit. They need a proper assessment to see if they need statementing, obviously, which I'd bet my bottom dollar they all do. And it needs doing as a matter of priority, in my view. Not only so we can get the extra funding we need to support them, but also because this has been overlooked for far too long already.'

'You're telling me!' I said.

'Anyway, as you know, they have their LAC review next week, so I just thought I'd let you know my recommendations. I'll obviously be bringing all this up then.'

I felt really happy after speaking to Julia. At last, I thought, at long last things were starting to happen. And not a moment too soon for these poor little ones. People think it's just a cliché to talk of children 'languishing' in care, but, to my mind, if they weren't getting the psychological and educational support they needed, that was *exactly* what kids like these two were doing. So what if Anna got her knickers in a twist about protocols? I didn't care. I'd come into fostering to do my bit to *stop* that. And that's what I intended to do.

A Looked After Children (LAC) review is a periodic meeting, held to discuss the situation and progress of a child (or sibling group) who is placed in the care system. It is run by an independent reviewer, and its purpose is to review the situation as it stands and to put in any plans for the future. Everyone involved with the child is invited, from foster carers, link workers and social workers, to the child or children's teachers and nurses, and, if family contact is a part of the arrangement, the parents as well.

The next scheduled meeting for Ashton and Olivia was to be held at their school the following Wednesday. And, in the meantime, as was the requirement, I had been busy writing our report. As foster carers, we were asked to update everyone else at the meeting, about both the progress that had been made since the last LAC review, as well as any ongoing concerns we wanted to raise.

'Got your list?' Mike asked, as we parked the car in the school car park. He'd booked a half-day's leave from work to attend with me. I didn't know then what a big thing this would be – he didn't always – I was just glad to have him with me so we could present a united front. And I was feeling pretty positive about things anyway.

'Sure have,' I said, waving it across the roof of the car as I climbed out. I had made a point of dressing smartly (as had Mike) – power dressing, if you like – as I wanted to impress upon the people that were present that we were professionals, and that our views needed hearing. 'And you know what?' I continued. 'Now I've written it all down, it's really made me focus on how much progress they've made. I really feel quite proud of them, to be honest.'

'And so you should be,' Mike said, squeezing my shoulder as we set off across the car park and into school. 'I mean, I know we're still battling with some pee and poo problems, but when you compare how they are now to how they were when they first came to us ... I almost wish we'd taken photos – you know – before and after. Easy to forget that they were practically feral! So you have every right to be proud, love.'

'And you too,' I reminded him, as we entered.

I don't know if it was a case of pride coming before a fall, but I did go into that meeting feeling we'd been doing a good job. The fact that there was so much still to do didn't matter. I had a spring in my step and I expected it to stay there. And now we had Dr Shackleton and Julia Styles on board too, I even thought it might get a little springier.

But that was before the meeting started.

Barbara, the school receptionist, who I'd known a long time, was the one to greet us. 'Coffee and biscuits right there,' she said, pointing. 'Then just head on in. Everyone's in there.'

We did as requested and entered a room full of people. I'd been to lots of LAC reviews and this one was a biggie, and as we took the seats John Fulshaw had reserved for the two of us, I scanned the room, seeing some unfamiliar faces. There were the expected ones, John and Anna, of course, and a quartet of school officers I recognised – the head of school, the school nurse, the family support worker and nurture room teacher – but also three people that I didn't. It was the first of these, Emma, the reviewing officer, who introduced the others, who turned out to be the head of the children's previous primary school, and a young woman who, we were told, was a teaching assistant there. They'd been asked along, Emma told us, because as the children's previous teachers, it was felt that their input and insights might be valuable.

Introductions over, Emma then went around the group, soliciting input, which Mike and I kicked off, outlining where the children had made improvements, but also reiterating how important we continued to feel it was that they get some sort of counselling as a matter of urgency.

I also added that, having spoken to Julia the previous week, I was pleased to see that the school were like-minded in this regard, in terms of urgent assessment of their special educational needs, probable statementing (the process of formally giving children a statement of special educational needs) and resultant extra support, so they could be placed within the right learning environment.

So far, I thought, once I'd said my piece, so good. With Julia behind me – she had nodded and murmured approval throughout – I felt we might finally see a bit more action. And so far the rest of the attendees had listened passively. It was only when the staff at the current school began relating their update that I felt the first stirrings of an atmosphere developing.

It seemed there was a theme developing, too, as, one by one, all the staff had their say, all expressing concern about the hindrance to progress as a result of the fact that the kids' 'very obvious' difficulties had not been picked up on before.

'Olivia's use of language and slightly strange ways, for example,' Julia said.

'Can you elaborate?' Emma wanted to know.

Julia could. 'She uses some strange language,' she said. 'And has a slightly odd manner and general demeanour. Then there are the bouts of hyperactivity, and the bouts of arm flapping that often accompany it. These are clearly longstanding behaviours that have become reinforced over time and need addressing as a priority. I also wonder if she needs her medication reassessed, as the ADHD is clearly still a factor.'

Next up was the school nurse, who expressed her agreement, but was able to add a positive about both children's weight gain, which had, since they'd been with us, come along nicely, with both of them being now within the correct boundaries for their age.

Emma duly noted all this down, together with Anna's testimony that the council were doing all they could to find permanent placements, as well as outlining their decision to split Ashton from Olivia, and why. This still upset me, of course, even though I understood the reasoning, and I had by now come to accept, however sadly, that the truth was that we didn't live in a utopia.

But the sadness was suppressed by a warm glow of positivity as John rounded up that part of the meeting.

'I think we can all agree,' he said, smiling in Mike and my direction, 'that the Watsons – who, I might add, were only supposed to have these two very short term – have been doing an exemplary job. And that's *without* the support they could have done with,' he added. 'As you all know, as temporary carers, they have no input from CAMHS, so apart from the support of the school, which has been excellent, they really have been going it alone.'

Was it that, I wondered afterwards, that so rankled with the other teachers? All I knew was that from that point on things became unpleasant. We moved straight on, then, to looking at an action plan for the immediate future, and it was at this point that the two of them were asked to contribute, to add their insight into the root of the children's problems. But we were all in for something of a shock.

I'd spoken briefly to Julia, of course, about the lack of documentation she'd been sent, but it seemed that was the tip of the iceberg.

The children's previous headmaster, Mr Moore, cleared his throat noisily, and proceeded to make something of a speech. 'I'm very pleased we've been asked to come here today,' he began. 'Because the extended family have been known to our school for a long time, and this latest pair did and do mean a lot to us. We taught both of them, right from reception class on and, as I say, knew the family extremely well. Educationally,' and here he paused and scanned the faces around the table, 'I must say I am surprised by what I've heard here today. According to *our* records, and from what I remember of the children personally, both children were perfectly capable at school. We never had problems with them.'

You could have heard a pin drop at that point, which I felt sure was what he intended, such was the tone of his words. I glanced at Julia, whose expression of shock mirrored mine. 'Really?' she said, her professional hackles up now. 'I have to say, I am somewhat surprised at that. We have conducted a lot of tests and are a hundred per cent certain that both children have a degree of learning disability. We will, of course, bring in the educational psychologist to re-affirm this, but they definitely require learning support.'

Had a pin dropped now, it would still make a clatter in the ensuing silence, as Mr Moore turned to his assistant. 'Well, Ann here,' he said, gesturing to the now nervous-looking woman sitting beside him, 'is the teaching assistant attached to the classes of both Ashton and Olivia and she assures me –' he smiled and she bobbed her head slightly – 'that there was never a problem with the children. They were always hard-working, quiet and friendly. There was nothing to suggest they needed extra support. The only worry we *did* have, was for Olivia and her rather "quaint" ways.'

'Which wasn't documented,' Julia shot back immediately.

'If you'll let me *finish*,' Mr Moore said. 'I was going to say that we were about to bring in a therapist when the children were removed from the school. But apart from that, we saw no evidence to concern us.'

'That's right,' added Ann, who appeared to have found her voice now. 'They were always adequately presented, and –'

It was at this point that perhaps she wished she hadn't.

'Adequately *presented*?!' This was Mike, who, up to now, had been silent, but his voice was as explosive as it was sudden. I could see he was aghast. '*Adequately presented*? Are we talking about the same family here? These are kids that were brought to us without any clothing to speak of, filthy dirty, heads ridden with lice! They the ones? Oh, and covered in scabies, too. The same kids, right?'

I placed my hand over Mike's on the table. He was livid – that was clear – and I could understand why. These people who professed to know these children so well didn't seem to know them at *all*. Could they even bring them to mind now? I seriously doubted it. I decided to speak before my husband blew a gasket.

'Mike's right,' I said, trying to keep my voice level. 'And, actually, our records indicate that the school – *your* school –' I looked pointedly at Mr Moore here – 'had sent a report to social services, saying pretty much the same. That they were unkempt most of the time, and hungry as well. And that they'd been caught stealing food from other children's lunch boxes, and the school rubbish bins, too, as I recall. Also, as far as their learning capacity goes, we all believe –' I glanced at Julia here, and she nodded – 'that they are at least a couple of years behind their peers. At *least*.'

Ann, the teaching assistant, smiled at me sweetly. 'Oh, I'm sorry, Mrs Watson,' she said softly. 'I didn't realise you were a teacher.'

I hated that it happened, but I felt my cheeks redden, as the sarcasm in her voice reached my ears.

'Actually, Ms Phelps,' I said, glancing at her name on the agenda, my heart beginning to thump against my ribcage, 'I *do* have a teaching degree, if that's any of your business. But that's irrelevant to what I'm telling you about these children. You don't need a teaching qualification to back up what I'm saying, which is that these children clearly have problems which have been manifest for *years*.'

I was fuming. I had no idea why this woman so had it in for me. I'd never met her, never slighted her. What was going *on* here? Was it just because the children had been removed from their school? Was *that* it?

'I'm sorry,' said Mr Moore again, filling the space his assistant's shocked silence had created. 'But I, um, we, have to disagree with your evaluation. And I'd like it to be noted that, as a school, we feel that if the children have now deteriorated, then maybe … well, maybe the current carers have let that side of things slide somewhat.'

Mike slammed his hands down on the table so hard that I almost jumped out of my skin. 'How DARE you!' he railed at the head teacher. 'How dare you! How dare you insinuate that we don't know our job! I tell you what, mate, if *you* had done your job properly, these kids might have been spared one hell of a lot of suffering and grief! In my opinion, *you* have contributed to that, you hear me?' He turned to me then. 'Are you okay, love?' His face was grey.

I was on the verge of tears now. So stunned by what had happened that I couldn't speak. Had the man actually said that? That *we* had made the children deteriorate? It was as ridiculous a suggestion as I'd heard in my life, but, even so, I felt cornered. Judged. In the headlights. How could he even suggest such a thing?

John stood up. He looked every bit as shocked as I felt. 'Emma,' he said. 'Would you mind if we called a halt? Ten minutes, okay? I'd like to have a word with Mike and Casey.'

She nodded, looking relieved, and the three of us trooped out.

Out in the corridor, Mike was as angry as ever. 'Honestly, Case, I could go right back in there and ... God! I can't believe what they're trying to insinuate!'

John nodded his agreement. 'Mike, I'm as gobsmacked as you are. But you know how these things can get – emotions run high. Everyone's under pressure. Things get heated ... You okay, Casey?'

I nodded. 'I'm fine. I'm just furious! How could he? And that *woman*! And after everything we've done for the kids! What the hell is her agenda? She sat right through the bloody meeting! She heard what was said. How can she come out with that? Honestly, John, I felt like slapping her one!'

'I could see that,' said Mike, making a concerted effort to calm down. He managed a thin smile. 'Which is why I thought I'd better step in for you.'

Seeing Mike regaining his temper reminded me I should do likewise. There was nothing to be gained by getting so het up. I took a deep breath and let it stream out through my nostrils.

'I'm okay now,' I said. 'I'm just fine.'

'Well, I'm not!' said John. 'Look, you just say the word, Casey, and I'll go right on back in there, this very minute, and tell them that's that. Placement over. I won't have any member of my team spoken to in that fashion! Just say the word and I'll go back and tell the whole bloody lot of them that that's it. That you've had enough. That you won't be spoken to like that. That they'll have to find an emergency placement elsewhere. *Today*!'

'John, come on. It wasn't really Anna's fault –' I began.

He shook his head. 'Makes no difference. She should have spoken up for you. *I* should have spoken up for you.'

Mike put a hand on his shoulder. 'Come on. You hardly had a chance, John.'

'Even so, I should have. Honestly, both of you, just say the word. If you've had enough, just say. I'll go and tell them."

I looked at Mike. Mike looked back. We didn't need to say anything. I had no idea how such a bizarre conversation had come about. But one thing was for sure. On the strength of what had clearly come before, these kids needed people like us in their corner. 'No way,' I said firmly. 'No *way*.'

Chapter 17

I brooded about that meeting all week. After we'd left it, John had agreed with Mike and I that there was something going on, that there was something we didn't know, and that he was determined to get to the bottom of it.

Several days passed, however, before he did as he'd promised; but he came good. Instead of phoning to tell me, or emailing, he turned up unexpectedly, just after the school run.

'Surprise!' he said cheerfully, as I gawped to see him standing there. 'Well, come on, let me in then,' he said. 'I have news!'

'Was I expecting you?' I asked him, trying to flick through a mental filing cabinet, wondering if there was an appointment I'd forgotten about.

'No, of course you weren't!' he said. 'The clue's in the word "surprise", Casey. Now let me in, will you, woman? It's brass monkeys out here!'

I made him a hot drink and allowed him to thaw for a few minutes before pestering him to put me out of my misery. 'So what *is* this news?'

He pulled a slim folder from his briefcase. 'Hold your horses,' he said. 'First up, here's the LAC review minutes. All fine, nothing to worry about. Pretty straightforward stuff.' He placed them on the kitchen table. 'You can read them at your leisure. My *real* news, however, is more edifying.'

This was what I'd been waiting for. 'Go on.'

'Well, as you can probably imagine all too well, I was still bloody livid when I got back to my office, so I decided to do a bit of detective work right away. Detective work on the school, following my gut instinct – which I trust – about just how "friendly" the school had actually been with the family. I mean, unless we had a case of pretty serious crossed wires, my understanding was that the school, though they clearly never intervened, *did* file a report when social services got involved and discussed plans to put the children into care.'

I nodded. 'Yes, they did. Anna said so.'

'Exactly. And they definitely *did* make reference to the kids being unkempt. And they definitely *did* make reference to them stealing out of bins.'

'I know,' I said. 'I saw it. Which means –'

'– that the head, Mr Moore, was talking rubbish, agreed?'

'Well, exactly! God, don't do this to me, John – spill!'

'And now I know why.' He paused, for effect, and sipped his coffee. 'So, earlier this year, that same school had their

OFSTED inspection. And OFSTED, of course, are the governing body that go in to check that a school is performing to the standards laid down in the National Curriculum, and –'

'John …'

'Oops!' he said, looking suddenly sheepish. 'Sorry, I keep forgetting you used to work in education. But anyway,' he leaned forward and whispered theatrically, 'the results, in this case, were atrocious. The school were told, and in no uncertain terms, it would seem, that they had only so many months to clean up their act before they would officially be put in special measures. OFSTED apparently targeted lots of different areas, but for the purposes of shedding light on what happened at that meeting, the main one of interest is in pastoral care. So my guess – no, more than a guess, I was damned damned certain – was that a finger pointing towards evidence of apathy towards these children was exactly what they didn't, and don't, need right now.'

I sat back, feeling a small glow of vindication. It all fell into place now. 'No, I can see that. They definitely wouldn't. No wonder they were so keen to try and lay the blame elsewhere.' I sat forward too, now. '*And* in circumstances where it would definitely be minuted. And so on record. Well of all the bloody cheek!'

'I know. But don't worry. I've phoned the head myself and drawn his attention to the original report. And I've also let my personal suspicions be known. He's not happy about it, obviously, but neither is he stupid. He's basically admitted that perhaps he wasn't suitably prepped before the meeting, and that "perhaps" – oh, how I loved that "perhaps"! – he'd not managed to read all the relevant paperwork first. The upshot is that he has now agreed he'll look into it and has also agreed – following my, erm, "directive" on the matter – that he'll prepare us a more accurate written report, which we can obviously attach to these minutes.'

'Sounds like you went in pretty hard, then.'

'I sure did.'

'And I'm really grateful, John. I can't tell you. Not that I'm not still bloody angry at the pair of them. It's so unprofessional! Fancy them putting the needs of those kids second – not to mention our reputation – to the saving of their own arses!'

'But no more. It'll all be down in there' – he pointed to the folder – 'in black and white. So that no fingers get pointed towards you and Mike. And quite right. The least I could do.'

'And as I said, I'm really grateful. Mike too, when I tell him. Though it shouldn't have been bloody necessary in the first place, should it?'

He shook his head. 'No, it shouldn't. But, hey ho. Such is life, eh? Anyway,' he said, draining his mug. 'Better get off. See you in a week or so, no doubt.' He stood up then, and I followed him back out into the hall, reaching past him to open the front door. The postman had been, so I picked up the letters from the mat while I was at it.

'Ooh,' I said, spying a bright-red envelope among them. 'First Christmas card! Anyway, thanks again, John. We really do appreciate your support.'

'You're welcome, Casey, you know that. Oh, but just the one thing,' he added, pointing towards the envelope. 'It's 1 December. Please, please don't let me come back here next week and find this place already trimmed up to the bloody nines! With my workload this month, I might just have to kill you.'

'John, I can't think *what* you mean!' I said, grinning.

So it was that, on 2 December, the run-up to Christmas properly started. I spent the next few days nagging Mike to go into the loft and get the decorations down, and didn't give him a minute's peace until he did. And it was all John's fault, I thought to myself, grinning. In truth, I hadn't even really thought of the 'C' word until he'd seen that card and brought it up on my doorstep. Now it felt almost obligatory to have the place done out like Santa's grotto before he next came.

But who was I kidding? It would only have been a matter of days anyway, because Christmas is my very favourite time of year. In my eyes there is nothing as glamorous in the world as an overdressed Christmas tree forming the centre piece of a house dripping with tinsel and fairylights. Curmudgeonly John or no (and I knew him well enough now to enjoy winding him up about it), I was always the first on our street to put up my glitzy decorations, both inside the house and outside. Indeed, there'd been years in the past when I'd have the stuff out of the loft almost the minute the last Bonfire Night firework had fizzled out, and would make a start on creating my window dressings. As the children got older, I had become a little less manic, but then along came the foster kids, and Levi, and, well … let's just say that I had long since learned to misinterpret the shaking heads of passers-by. I preferred to imagine that what they were thinking as they passed was, 'There she goes again! And good on her! That woman is just *so* dedicated to Christmas!'

Not that I was entirely democratic about the decorations. Though I always promised the children they could help to trim the tree, I was a one-man band when it came to the rest of the house, a job I traditionally liked to have done and truly dusted before the schools broke up and everything got so hectic.

It was funny what a turnaround I'd experienced in that regard. When I worked in schools myself, like everyone else, I used to love the school holidays. But now, I guess, like millions of other parents across the country, it felt like the schools always seemed to be on holiday! It would certainly feel like a pretty long three weeks this year.

Though this wasn't just selfishness on my part. Just lately – well, increasingly over the last few weeks, if I was honest – the children's behaviour, particularly in regard to their ADHD, seemed to becoming more evident. And in the midst of that, it was becoming increasingly hard to maintain a calm home environment. Olivia, in particular, was becoming trying. Having the school draw attention to some of her over-excited behaviour seemed to make me notice it with greater frequency. And she really did remind me of an over-excited little bird when her medication levels dipped, as she'd run around and then jump up, perching on the backs of chairs, crouching, and then leaping onto anyone who passed by. She was affectionate with it, but she'd still scare everyone half to death, and I knew it really needed addressing.

But when she wasn't hyper, she often seemed to be miles away, and I knew she was still being regularly ambushed by feelings of homesickness – particularly for her granddad. And for the rest of her family. And perhaps the reality of that permanent separation was sinking in. Necessary, I knew, but so sad.

But of the two of them, it was Ashton who concerned me the most. He was definitely becoming more aggressive. Since the incident at the party – perhaps something had come to a head? – he had become more irritable, and seemed to like taking it out on his little sister, pushing her around and pulling her hair till she cried. And no matter how much I tried to talk to him about it, he seemed to have this default setting called 'angry and defiant', which was showing no signs of going away.

I had no real idea why this was. Did their medication need changing or was this simply the real deal? Was it actually indicative that the children were now so settled that they no longer felt they had to be on 'best' behaviour? As any parent knows, the most sorted kids generally have an emotionally healthy system; they know how to behave and generally do behave in company, and save their worst behaviours for the place where they feel most secure, which, in most 'normal' families, is home and mother. If that was so, then perhaps I should embrace it as a positive. But I wasn't sure. I just hoped Dr Shackleton would come through and we could start to get to the root of who these children really were and, more importantly, what they could become. I also recalled that Justin, who'd come to us just before Christmas three years ago, found the whole thing a terrible strain. Coming from a home where he was not only lacking food and care, but also love – his mother didn't have an ounce of love for him inside her – Christmas, I thought, looking back with the benefit of hindsight, just underlined that tragic fact tenfold.

But these kids had each other, and also perceived themselves as loved (even if it was the sort of love that should see some of the adults concerned behind bars), so I felt certain, and determined, that their Christmas at our house would be a wonderful time for them all.

Within a fortnight, and with the end of the winter term fast approaching, I'd pretty much done everything bar the tree itself. And on the Friday I'd spent much of the day tackling the living room – the room which I always left decorating till last, as it was the focal point of the whole house. I was so engrossed that I was almost late picking up the kids from school, deciding at the last minute that I'd switch off all the house lights, plunging the place into darkness – well, by the time we came home from school, it *would* be dark – so that I could usher them all in and do the big 'reveal', switching all the fairy lights on, and creating magic.

Accordingly, I had them troop in, still in their coats, and

made them stand in the doorway while I went to the socket that powered my biggest multi-plug adaptor.

'Ta-da!' I said, as the room was suddenly alive with coloured twinkles. Even without the tree, it still looked pretty gorgeous.

Olivia spoke first. 'It's really pretty,' she said, sounding not so much excited as bewildered. 'It's really lovely. What's it for?'

'Because soon it will be Christmas, sweetie, and I really like to make it look pretty for Christmas. And over there' – I pointed to the space I'd prepared in the corner – 'is where we're going to put the Christmas tree.'

At the mention of the tree, Olivia did at least seem to register the coming occasion.

'D'you want to help me with that after tea?' I asked Ashton. 'Did you used to help Mummy with her tree?'

'Yeah, an' it was better than your tree,' said Ashton, shocking me. He stuck out his lower lip and glared at me. What I'd said had clearly hit a nerve.

Feeling deflated now, I almost said, 'How would you know? You haven't seen *my* tree yet!', but managed to bite it back just in time. This would be the first Christmas these kids had spent anywhere but home. Their emotions about it would be complex.

'Oh, don't be such a meany pants,' Olivia interrupted on my behalf. 'It'll be lovely. Can I help as well, Casey?'

'You can *both* help,' I told them. 'That's what I want. For you both to help me. Right after tea, yes? Now come on. Sausage and mash and mushy peas coming up.'

About which they seemed *much* more excited. As with beaches, I reflected, so with Christmas. It was as if they couldn't quite see the point.

As it turned out, Olivia did help me decorate the tree – Ashton mostly sat on the sidelines, looking scornful – but it was a half-hearted effort. So much so that it occurred to me that far from worrying about them getting too over-excited, I'd struggle to get them excited at all. And it was a theme that was set to continue.

As the days ticked by, I began planning my present-buying sorties, and was concerned I didn't know what to get them both. I tried asking them what they'd like, but neither of them seemed to have a clue. They just didn't seem to understand the concept. They understood getting birthday presents, clearly – we'd seen that with them, at least – but when I tried to put myself into the shoes of the wretched young girl who was their mother, I wondered if it was simply a case of, if you couldn't do it properly, why do it at all? So much easier to forget the whole business.

But completely? Not even so much as a tangerine and a few nuts and chocolate coins in an old sock? I did mention it to Anna when she called, to see if she had any thoughts on it, because, much as I tried to understand it, their total lack of engagement with something as normal as getting and giving presents for loved ones at Christmas was completely outside my experience. Not that she could really shed any light on it. She just told me that as far as she knew they'd just never really 'done' Christmas. There was no money, and with so many kids in the family it just hadn't ever really happened.

So perhaps my initial feeling had been right. And if there was an illustration of how far things had come in our civilised society, that was it, I thought. That in the absence of money, Christmas couldn't be 'done'. As if Christmas was even about that! It was certainly a sobering thought. And one I should take on board too, I thought, rapidly re-adjusting my perspective. I'd worked in school with a child whose parents were Jehovah's Witnesses. She hadn't 'done' Christmas either. And what you'd never had you didn't miss, did you? And perhaps that was no bad thing.

Even so, to quote Jo from *Little Women* on the subject, Christmas wouldn't be Christmas without any presents, so, even with the true meaning of Christmas still very much in mind, I wanted to get some for my little charges. And, crucially, things they'd really like. And handily, with Lauren having now broken up from college, she and Kieron were happy to help out.

They were around for the afternoon and, at Kieron's suggestion, suggested they while away an hour with the kids, going through a couple of copies of the Argos catalogue to get some ideas for what to ask Father Christmas for.

'Here we go,' said Kieron, patting the chair beside him. 'Ash, come on. Come sit beside me – and we can have a go-through and check out all these brilliant boys' toys, while Lauren and Olivia' – and here he pulled a comedy face at Olivia – 'look at all the silly soppy girly stuff.'

Lauren returned the compliment as I handed out pens and paper. 'Come on,' she said, 'let's make a nice long list for Santa of all the things you'd like him to bring on Christmas Day.'

'Erm,' I said, before leaving them. 'Not *too* long a list! Santa's only got so much space in his sleigh!'

Though actually I needn't have worried. Even with Kieron and Lauren to guide them, the kids didn't seem to have the first idea about coveting a really special toy. They ticked things off politely, but without any great enthusiasm. They just didn't seem to want *anything*.

'It's funny,' I said to Riley, who was over a few days later. 'Such a shocking and tragic upbringing and almost every way, and yet, to some people, these kids would seem like a dream. How many kids in the western world these days are as genuinely non-materialistic as these two, do you think?

'I know,' she said. 'I can't get my head round it, really. You'd think, what with school, talking to their peers and all that stuff, that they'd have at least *some* idea of what they've missed out on. But they really don't, do they?'

I shook my head. 'I know. And it's not that I want them to become materialistic, either. It just feels so sad. They must have grown up so isolated, mustn't they?'

Riley shot me a knowing glance. 'I don't doubt it. If you want to abuse your kids on the sort of scale that family clearly have, I'd say it probably goes with the territory, doesn't it? Anyway,' she added, 'since we're speaking of Christmas, there's something I meant to ask you. Well, tell you, more accurately.'

'What?' Riley was only eight or so weeks from her due date, and my thoughts, seeing as she looked so serious all of a sudden, went immediately to her unborn baby.

'Don't look so anxious!' she laughed. 'It's nothing terrible. Though it will be a shock ...'

'*What*, for God's sake?!'

'I'm doing Christmas lunch, okay? Over at mine. You'll have enough on your plate with those two to run around after, and you'll be grateful to have someone else cook for you, trust me.'

'Riley, you're thirty-two weeks pregnant!'

'Yes, *pregnant*. Not ill. And I've made up my mind.'

'Absolutely not!' I said firmly.

Naturally, my daughter being even feistier than I was, Christmas Day at hers was duly arranged. It felt weird, waking up and not having to think about the turkey, but she'd been right. Once I thought about it, it *was* the right thing. After all, little Levi was two now. Probably time they started making their own family Christmas memories for him. And Riley had been spot-on about my little foster duo, too. It would be good to spend some quality time with them without having an enormous roast dinner to prepare.

But there was another big difference to that Christmas morning. When I woke – I'd set my alarm for 5 a.m. – the house was as silent as a grave. And as I crept downstairs in my dressing gown and lit the gas fire in the living room I thought back to all the years when my own children had been young, and a 5 a.m. alarm call would have been a luxury. One year Kieron was by our bed trying to shake us awake only about an hour after we'd dropped off to sleep!

I put the television on, and found a channel playing Christmas songs, and flicked all the fairy lights on too. And as I placed the two bulging sacks at either end of the sofa, I decided that if there was one thing I could do for them it would be to give them a magical family Christmas to remember, because memories like those really mattered.

The scene set, and a surprised Bob put out into the garden to do his business bright and early, I padded back upstairs in the darkness and gently shook Olivia awake. 'He's been!' I whispered to her, picking her up. 'Santa's been and left you presents!'

'But I peed,' she whispered sleepily. 'Will Santa be cross with me?'

I stood her on the bed and peeled off her wet pyjamas. 'No, of course not,' I reassured her. 'Santa's never cross. He's Santa! He knows accidents happen,' I added, pulling a clean set of pyjamas from her drawer. 'Quick, let's pop these on. We can give you a bath later. Let's go and wake Ashton now so we can all go downstairs.'

Once woken, Ashton stumbled blearily into his dressing gown, and as the two children followed me down the stairs, I could already tell that I was probably more excited than they were; in fact, they must have been wondering what on earth I was doing, dragging them out of bed at such a crazy hour.

In fact, they didn't really 'get' anything about it. 'Go on, get stuck in!' I urged, as they knelt by their sacks and I perched on the sofa with a steaming mug of coffee, and turning up the volume of the TV a notch or two, tried to inject a little extra festive atmosphere.

But it was pointless. They'd each open a present, as directed, inspect it, then look at me blankly. It was as if they were being asked to do a task in the classroom, with a beady-eyed teacher looking on. There was no frantic tearing off of wrapping paper, no excited oohs and ahhs, no shouts of glee as a much wanted toy was revealed. It was, in fact, one of the saddest things I'd witnessed, as I realised that this wasn't any sort of thrill for them at all. They were just trying to do what I wanted, to make me happy. Ashton, in particular, upset me. He'd been so gruff and so grumpy and so closed in since Levi's party, but I could tell he was aware how much Christmas seemed to mean to me, and his attempts to please me by thanking me so politely for each new gift actually made tears spring in my eyes.

It was with pretty dampened spirits, then, that we set off for Riley's mid-morning. Mike had got up and joined us, and we'd tucked into breakfast, and I'd told him that the children had been ever so excited and thrilled with all the lovely things Santa had brought them, because there was no point in infecting him with my own gloomy mood. I'd cheer up, I knew, once I clapped eyes on Levi. And Olivia, at least, had become attached to one of her presents. A new dolly, which she dressed up and brought along with her and, entirely predictably, called 'Polly'.

'Another Polly?' asked Mike as she pulled the doll's hood up.

Olivia looked at him as if he'd recently beamed down from space. '*All* dollies are called Polly, Mike,' she explained patiently. 'Polly wolly doodle doll a day.'

Since this made no sort of sense to Mike (or, in fact, me) he simply nodded.

'There,' she said, tucking the doll beneath the blanket in her little buggy. 'All done. Now she and Liccle Levi can play babies, all ready.'

'All ready for what?' Mike wanted to know, as we tramped down the front path, and along the frosty pavements so that Bob could inspect every lamppost. At least the weather had played ball and made everything sparkly.

Olivia tutted. 'All ready for the *real* baby, silly! Don't you *know* Wiley's gonna have a babba, Mike?'

But if that put a smile on my face that Christmas morning, I would soon see it replaced by a bigger one. Riley's front door was opened not by Riley, but by Santa. A six-foot four Santa, pink cheeked and jolly, yelling 'ho ho ho!' from behind a luxurious white beard. This, at least, did seem to galvanise the kids into excitement. Olivia, dolly now entirely forgotten, shrieked delightedly and wrapped herself straight around Santa's leg.

And it galvanised me too, because I could see it wasn't David. And it wasn't Kieron either, so who *was* it? The beard was whipped off then, and it was me who was screaming. It was Justin, our first ever foster child! I was so thrilled to see him that I practically leapt on him. But didn't need to. He carefully extricated Olivia, then picked me up and spun me right around. 'Steady on, Casey!' he quipped, putting me down again gently. 'Size of you, you nearly knocked me clean over!'

I couldn't have been happier if it had been Santa himself. Actually, that was wrong. I just couldn't have been happier. And Justin, that poor, desperate boy who had become so dear to us, was the catalyst that turned the day around. Now 14, he immediately mesmerised the children, particularly Ashton, who seemed to hang on his every word. Not that there was much time for sitting down and chatting; right away he had the three of them – little Levi wasn't missing out on *anything* – playing games and having fun, chasing them around the house as if he was still 10 years old himself.

And our own children, unbeknown to us, had arranged everything. They'd squared it with social services, spoken directly to Justin's foster carers, and David and Kieron had gone and picked him up that morning.

The children couldn't have got me a nicer present.

Chapter 18

It had been such a delight to see Justin. He made the day in every sense, for all of us. He had us in stitches, telling us tales of his various exploits at school, and also surprised us by helping Riley cook Christmas dinner. Not that I should have been surprised, as he'd been quite the budding Jamie Oliver when he'd been with us, always wanting to help me in the kitchen, and his interest in food and cooking clearly hadn't gone away. I really hoped that he was as happy as he seemed and that he'd remain settled in his permanent placement.

It was the thing I most wanted for Justin; that he'd be happy. It was the thing I most wanted for every child who came into our lives, and in the immediate aftermath of Christmas I felt particularly buoyed up; it might not seem much, all the little things we could do for these kids, but it felt more and more to me that it was the little things that mattered, things which weren't always obvious while the child or children were with us. A word of encouragement, taking the time to sit and listen to them, a random cuddle, a special cake made, a fear soothed, an anxiety understood: these were the things kids who were loved and nurtured took for granted, and their importance should never be underestimated.

And they *did* make a difference; Justin was evidence of that. A timely reminder that progress with a child wasn't always evident when being made – you were often too close to it – but down the line, even if Mike and I wouldn't be there to see it, I felt a strong sense that the results of our efforts would at least be there for the kids' permanent carers to witness.

Assuming they found any; progress on that front was painfully slow. But strangely, I didn't mind at all. In fact, I started the year with a real zest to keep on doing what we were doing with our two. Just as well, for there was still a great deal to be done.

I was still anxious about how Ashton was coping with the loss of everything and, bar just one of his younger siblings, everyone he knew. Where Olivia, as the baby, seemed the least traumatised by their big life-change (despite her odd behaviours, and sadness about leaving Grandad, she was by nature a sunny little thing and, with love and support, I knew could be again), Ashton, being the oldest, was really feeling it. He clearly loved his mother dearly, and was always her staunch defender, determined not to break the thread of connection between them, knowing all too well he'd not see her again for a long time. He would not hear a word said against her by his sibling, even if it was something that was only implied.

And it could be triggered in unexpected ways.

'School tomorrow,' I was telling the children, a couple of days after New Year, while we were packing the last of the decorations into the loft boxes. 'I'll bet you can't wait, can you? To get back and swap stories with all your friends.'

'I like having friends,' Olivia said, as she popped baubles into trays. 'I like Emily. An' Scarlett. Scarlett's so funny!'

Ashton, sitting on his heels, was untangling a string of fairy lights. 'I *really* like having friends,' he said, thoughtfully.

'Me too,' I said. 'Life's not much fun without friends, is it? I mean, family's great, but you need friends as well, don't you?'

'We never had friends before because we was stinky,' observed Olivia. 'Cos we were stinky and nitty noras because of all our lices.'

Ashton rounded on her immediately. 'No!' he barked. 'That's not true! We weren't stinky and we never had nits neither, *okay*? Mum'd kill you – *and* Granddad – for saying bad things like that an' telling tales!'

'But we *were*,' she persisted.

'No we weren't! You're a liar!' With which he threw down the string of lights and marched angrily from the room.

'We *were*,' Olivia whispered defiantly, once he was out of earshot. 'He just doesn't member it, Casey. Cos he's a *boy*.'

* * *

But as the new year got under way, my anxiety about the children began to shift again, in intensity, towards Olivia. For all the comedy evident sometimes in her eccentric little ways, I knew I must never forget that they were, in part, manifestations of repeated sexual abuse. And she'd always been a particularly imaginative child, too, living a rich and varied life in her head.

I didn't know if it was just another manifestation of her becoming more settled with Mike and me, or the fact that there was one soon to be born into our family, but her fondness of all things pregnancy and baby related was becoming so intense as to begin to feel like an obsession.

And it wasn't Riley's impending baby, either. Out of the blue, Olivia started carrying on as if she truly believed she was pregnant too. She took to walking round the house with a football up her jumper, arching her back and moaning about her various aches and pains. It was amusing at first, particularly for Kieron – it was his football – when he was roundly told off for 'being cheeky, young man!' when he asked her if he could have his ball back. He was also in stitches, he told me, when he overheard her telling her assembled dolls that 'Mummy will feel like playing again, once this bloomin' baby is borned. Just a few more weeks, sweetheart.' She would also rush to the toilet, making vomiting noises and complaining about her 'bloomin' morning sickness'.

But it was her need for 'some exercise' that capped everything. She'd asked me if she could 'go out the front' one afternoon, after school, because she needed 'exercise, so I don't get too many stretch marks'. I agreed to this, on condition that, though she could certainly take the football, she wasn't allowed to wear it under her clothing.

She'd been out there half an hour or so – lots of the kids played out the front before tea – when I was alarmed to respond to a ring on the doorbell and find a police constable standing on the front step. Casting anxiously around for Olivia, and wondering what on earth had happened, I was relieved to see her sitting on next door's wall, clutching the football and looking bored. 'I just thought you should know,' the young policeman said, once we'd established I was her guardian, 'that I brought her home because she's behaving, well, let's say, a little bit oddly, and I just wanted to be sure she was all right.'

He went on to explain that he'd come across her around the corner, not joining in with the other children's games, but squatting on all fours on the pavement, wailing and groaning theatrically.

When he'd ask if she was okay she had apparently replied, 'No, I'm six months gone and my bloody waters have broke!' He'd naturally responded that that was a silly thing to say, and her response to that was to bark back, 'Oh, silly, is it? I'm bloody knackered! I've been up all night breastfeeding the twins!'

Trying hard to suppress the smile that kept threatening to overwhelm me, I assured him she was fine and that I'd bring her inside and have a word with her – though what he expected me to do (tick her off for frightening young constables?) I really didn't know. And I did call her in, and while I explained to her, for the umpteenth time, that grown-ups became concerned when she did her 'having a baby' acting, it occurred to me that my life had become quite surreal.

Not that it stopped her, in any case, because it was only a day later when she came down to breakfast sporting two big wet patches on her pyjama top. When Mike asked her what had happened she told him she'd been 'leakin' from me breasts', rubbing her 'sore titties' and groaning for good measure.

'It's not nice this, you know!' she said, seeing me staring. 'Can't you jus' gimme a tablet or somefink, Casey? Gawd, I'll be glad when this one's on the bottle an' can leave my poor titties alone!'

But for all my relief that her pregnancy obsession ended almost as abruptly as it started, it was replaced by one that felt much more sinister. Where we'd been amused by her antics as 'Mummy Olivia' her new obsession was no laughing matter. She developed a distinctly unsettling thing about fire.

Looking back, it had always been there in a mild form. She'd always been fascinated by the gas flames on my hob when I was cooking, seemingly mesmerised, talking about how beautiful they were, and how they almost looked like they were dancing. I'd always thought it strange, but, bar a sensible observance of safety, I had never let it bother me. I was also aware of what the kids had told me about the family car being torched. But out of the blue, or so it seemed, this had gone a stage further; watching one of the soaps one night, following a scene where a building had caught fire, she was rapt, watching the family trapped in an upstairs bedroom. 'Rewind it, Mike! Please! Can you play it again?' she pleaded. She hadn't taken her eyes off the screen.

'Rewind what?' Mike asked, not having really taken in what she was on about.

'The fire,' she explained. 'The bit where they all burn to death!'

'No-one's burned to death,' he said mildly, 'they're just trapped.' He grinned. 'We won't know if they burn to death till tomorrow now.'

'They will, though,' she said seriously. 'Oh, please. Go on, rewind it. There might be a clue we all missed. They'll all be dead, though, I think,' she added, matter of factly.

'Well, as I said,' Mike answered, looking at me now, his expression puzzled, 'we'll find out tomorrow, okay?'

'Enough telly anyway,' I said, anxious to get her off such a morbid subject.

'Okay,' she said brightly, jumping down off the sofa. 'Can I go on the computer instead?'

Ashton was playing in his bedroom at the time so, unusually, a laptop was free. I'd let Kieron borrow the other one to use at Lauren's. 'Course you can,' I said. 'Come on. Into the kitchen with me, then.'

She trotted happily behind me and I set up the laptop on the kitchen table, and she settled down happily, humming to herself, while I made a start on washing up the tea things.

'What're you playing?' I asked, as I glanced across the kitchen a minute later. Her little face was screwed up in concentration.

'Oh, just some-fing,' she said. 'Casey, d'you have earphones I could borrow?'

'I'm not sure where they are,' I said, drying my hands and going over. 'But you can just use the volume control anyway. Here, I'll show you ...'

I stopped as I realised what she was watching. Not porn. This time. No chance. Our security settings saw to that. No, it was an episode of something like *The Bill* in which, once again, there was a building burning down. The was a body bag on a stretcher being carried out by two firemen. What a strange thing for a little girl to want to watch. Particularly since she'd been so traumatised by fireworks. But then, I reasoned, that might have been more about the noise. This seemed to be more about the visual.

'You shouldn't be watching things like this, love,' I told her, reaching out to the track pad. 'It'll give you nightmares.'

'But it's my favourite bit!' she said. 'Oh, Casey, please don't turn it off!'

'It's not suitable,' I persisted.

'Can I watch *Casualty* instead, then?'

Another programme full of pain and death. Lovely. 'What's this fascination you've got with fires, love?' I asked her.

She shrugged. 'I don't know. I just like 'em. You know, fires and stuff and all that.' She looked at me with one of her old-fashioned expressions. 'People got to die, Casey, y'know. It's just one o' them things.'

So not just the sight of the pretty flames, then. She seemed fixated on the idea of violent death. I was beginning to be so troubled by all this that I phoned John Fulshaw the next morning and asked him what he thought. He'd dealt with scores of troubled kids over the years but was as clueless as I was. He did, however, try to reassure me. 'Probably just a phase,' he said. 'Working through her demons, I expect. I don't think you should draw too much attention to it; just monitor. Just encourage discussion generally. See if you can draw her out. It might disappear of its own accord. Probably will. As I said, just observe. Try not to worry.'

But I couldn't help *but* worry. It was as strange as it was gruesome, and as the days went by, showed no sign of letting up.

A few days later, in fact, it even seemed to be getting worse, when I made a pretty unsettling discovery in her bedroom, which seemed to confirm what I'd already thought. I'd gone up to strip and change the bed, and as I pulled the old bottom sheet out, I found a small pile of newspaper and magazine cuttings under the mattress. I could hardly credit it, but this seven-year-old who could barely concentrate for even a minute on her school reading book had secretly amassed a little cache of news items, every one of them about death and dying. One was about the soap we'd watched – from one of my magazines, no doubt – another was about a local businessman who'd dropped dead from a heart attack and another about a house fire that had claimed a whole family.

On this occasion I felt I must tackle her about it. Not confrontationally; just couched in the terms of a pleasant chat, about why she had created her small collection.

'I dunno,' she said. 'I just like cutting stuff out, and that.' And that was the only explanation I got out of her.

Further light was, however, shed just a day or so later, when I heard her asking Ashton how to spell 'disaster'. She was on the laptop at the time, painstakingly typing it into the search box as he called out the letters. 'Olivia!' I couldn't help saying. 'You have to stop this! It's unhealthy. Why on earth are you searching the word 'disaster'?'

She turned to me. 'Casey,' she said solemnly, 'you just never know. You never know when him upstairs is about to release his wrath. But he does, see, just you mark my words.'

Where the hell – *no*, I thought, not *where*, more like *who*? – had this little girl learned all this *from*?

Chapter 19

Only a couple of weeks after the birth of Olivia's 'baby', a new member of the Watson clan entered the world. The spitting image of his big brother, he was absolutely delightful, and lucky me, once again, got to be one of Riley's birth partners, helping welcome my new grandson into the world.

And Jackson was as obliging as he was gorgeous. I know most new mums would rather their babies came along at reasonably civilised hours, but getting the call from Riley at two in the morning was a godsend. It meant I could creep out of bed quietly and leave Mike and the kids sleeping; so much better for everyone than if it had happened in the middle of a busy day, with the kids needing babysitting and Mike off at work.

The labour, as is often the case with second ones, was quick. So by dawn, after an uncomplicated three hours, it was all over, and I was busy doing the traditional nanna thing at such moments, bawling my eyes out and congratulating my clever daughter. It was then that my phone bleeped. It was a text message from Mike, wanting to know how things were going, so, handing Jackson to his adoring daddy, I popped outside to call him.

'Oh, he's just gorgeous!' I gushed. 'Looks exactly like Levi! And Riley's positively glowing, and … well, it's just perfect. Anyway, love. All okay at home?'

'It's been better,' he admitted, adding a little laugh, for good measure. But I knew my husband well. He was trying not to puncture my happy mood. 'It's been better' meant things weren't good at all.

'What's happened, love?' I asked him, my mind immediately back-pedalling to Olivia's recent obsessions with fire and death.

'Nothing specific. They're both just being absolute nightmares. Don't know what's got into them! Well, I do. You not being there when they woke up, and why. Olivia, especially. Had to move mountains to get her pill down her. She's decided you don't want the pair of them anymore.'

'Oh, love. You poor thing. And you need to get off to work, don't you? Don't worry. Quick ciggie, then I'm on my way home, okay?'

'Appreciate it, love,' he said wearily.

After hanging up and having my quick fix inside the warmth of my car, I hurried back inside to say a quick farewell, and have a final cuddle with my new grandchild. It was only natural, I guessed, the kids kicking off, when you thought about it. A new baby was a time of change and upheaval in any family, but these two in particular must have found it particularly traumatic. A new baby, in their former lives, would almost certainly have meant an even greater degree of neglect – if that were possible. And, grim as it was to contemplate, an even more preoccupied and useless mother, leaving them prey to the kind of attention we knew they *did* get.

I stopped off at the supermarket on the way home, both to get a teddy bear for Jackson, and also to pick up two carefully chosen jigsaws and two big bars of chocolate as presents to give to Ashton and Olivia. It was all about making sure they were included in the happy event, so they didn't feel they were now being pushed away. That would be happening sooner rather than later in any case, I knew. But the physical parting would be managed so much better if their faith in our love for them, when they did leave, was secure.

But, jigsaws and chocolate and cuddles notwithstanding, it turned out I'd been horribly optimistic. Within minutes of arriving home I could see from their whole demeanour, that the arrival of this baby – and not even into the same household – had had a profound psychological effect. The whole of that week was a total nightmare. At a stroke, they seemed to have forgotten all the skills we'd so painstakingly taught them. They reverted back to their sloppy eating habits, their incessant inappropriate touching of one another and their toileting issues, always a bit rocky still with Olivia, just nosedived straight back down to the dark days. Every single day that week we had to deal with the aftermath, scrubbing underclothes or bedding or both.

And the same theme emerged every time I tried to sit down and reassure them. This – the new baby – had made it so clear. They couldn't be good enough, weren't loved enough, weren't nice enough children – why else were we sending them away?

It was so difficult to manage. And so upsetting. Up to now, and in my past job in the comprehensive school 'unit', I'd dealt with children old enough to understand the circumstances they'd been placed in. Even if they didn't like it, they understood that my and Mike's role was temporary; that we were a step on the road to a new life – not *the* life. But how could you tell these little ones that you loved them and cared for them, at the same time as telling them they had to go away? No matter how delicately social services dressed it up and had us deliver it, the message was one the kids simply couldn't understand.

'You know we gotta go somewhere else, Casey?' Ashton said to me one day after school. 'Well, how come they haven't got anyone for us yet?'

'I don't know, love,' I said, honestly. 'It's just that sometimes these things can take time.'

He looked right at me. 'But Casey, we've already been here for ages. So why can't we just stay with you?'

I wanted to hug him, but could sense that this wasn't the moment. He wanted a straight answer, not a platitude. 'Because me and Mike, love, well, we don't do long-term care. Our job is to love you and care for you – and we do love you both, *very* much – but only for a while, till they can find you a forever family.'

He frowned. 'Not forever.' I could have kicked myself. Wrong word. 'I'm off back to me mum's soon as I'm old enough. They can't stop me.'

His face was a picture of grim determination. 'Well, I guess that's fine, too,' I said. 'When you're old enough.'

Olivia, who'd been playing in the conservatory with Bob, now stood in the kitchen doorway. She's obviously heard us talking.

'Nobody likes us, do they, Casey?' she said, her eyes filling with tears.

'Oh, love,' I said, scooping her up and settling her on my knee. 'How could anyone not like you two?' I said, cuddling her. 'You're both beautiful. And funny and sweet and, well – you know how special you are to me. Anyone would be *proud* to have you go and live with them.'

Separately, of course, which thought made my stomach do a flip. I hated that they didn't know that was happening. But Anna had been firm that we mustn't prepare them. And she was right. It wouldn't help. Better to leave it till the last minute than have them distressed before they needed to be.

Olivia looked up at me, sniffing. 'Casey, from now on pwomise, okay? I pwomise that'll I'll be the bestest girl ever, so's the fost'ring people like me an' want me.'

'Me too,' said Ashton firmly. It broke my heart.

* * *

I called Anna the following day to see what progress was being made. The children's deterioration, since Jackson had come along, was a bit of a worry. I was keen to see them settled, however much I'd miss them, but the last thing I wanted was for some potential foster families to be found, only to refuse to take them because of this dip in their behaviours. But there was little to report anyway, which was what I'd half-expected. But at least they had pretty full profiles compiled for the children now, which were going to the social services panel on a fortnightly basis. It was the panel's job – being a team of experienced professionals within social services – to try to best-match potential carers with children. Now they were formally 'on the case' (which had been a long time in happening), it really was only a matter of time.

None of this meant anything to the children, of course. And there was no point in bringing the subject up, either. They lived in the here and now, which was how it needed to be. The only thing was that the here and now was in a state of mild chaos, as a result of their unsettled state.

And it was beginning to spill out of the house now. It was the following Saturday, a day I'd earmarked for some serious Casey-style cleaning, when I heard the doorbell ring, not once, but three times. It was one of our neighbours – one we didn't have much to do with – clutching the jumper of a fraught Olivia, who was wriggling frantically, trying to escape his grip.

'Oh!' I said, completely fazed by what was happening.

'Oh, indeed! I've just caught this dirty little oik in my front garden!'

Whatever the misdemeanour, his tone was horrible. 'Can you let her go, please?' I asked him crossly. 'You can see she's frightened, can't you? There's no need to man-handle her, whatever it is she's done!'

'Oh, that's right, is it?' he responded, equally crossly. 'You'd like me to squat down and take a shit on *your* front lawn, would you?'

I'm not sure I heard right. Or made sense of it, anyway. 'I beg your pardon,' said. 'What the hell are you on about?'

'This one!' he barked. 'Just pulled her fucking pants down and had a crap on my front lawn!'

If he'd been a touch less aggressive I might have apologised a touch more fulsomely. No, it wasn't a very nice thing to happen to anyone, but this was a small frightened child and my hackles had risen. 'Well, I'm very sorry,' I said, 'and I shall come and deal with that for you, but right now, I'll take things from here, thanks.' I shut the door.

Once it was closed I turned around. 'What on earth were you *thinking* of?' I asked Olivia. 'You *know* not to do that! You know you *mustn't do that*!'

She had no answer, of course. Just stood trembling there in front of me, twin streams of tears flowing down her pale cheeks. 'Go on,' I said. 'Up to your room. Scoot. Go up there and think about what I've told you about pooing. In the toilet. Nowhere else. In the *toilet*!'

There was no point in saying anything else to her right now. Later, perhaps. But not now. God, I thought, contemplating the grim task that awaited me in next door's front garden. Just how much worse were things going to get?

'Ask a silly question …' was the answer I got, an hour later. In the meantime I told myself to calm down. And give Olivia time to calm down a bit too, come to that, so I could sit down with her and try to have a rational conversation about why she'd felt the need to do what she'd done. Even with their lapses indoors, this was beyond my comprehension. I didn't think for a moment that she'd needed the toilet so badly that she couldn't make it home. Were that the case, she would surely just have soiled her pants. This was a deliberate act – God, when were these poor kids going to get some bloody counselling? – and that being so, just how much distress was she trying to convey, and how could we get her to find another way?

Mike had taken Ashton to watch a vintage-car rally that morning, and would be back within the hour, and I wanted this dealt with before they got home. I'd have a coffee, I decided – give it another fifteen minutes – then I'd go up and see how Olivia was doing and try to get her to open up to me about it. I was just pouring it when I became aware of some noise from upstairs; intermittent banging and scraping sounds and then, suddenly, an ear-splitting scream.

Banging the mug down, I raced up the stairs two at a time, but was then stopped in my tracks on the landing. It was the smell that hit me first, the whole upstairs smelled of faeces, so strongly that I even started gagging.

Placing my hand over my nose and mouth, I then entered her bedroom, taking in the scene found there as if watching some insane movie. The first thing I saw was the wall above Olivia's bed, on which was written in huge uneven letters, in red felt pen: 'AM EVUL. EVERY WON HAYTS ME.' Olivia, all the while, was screaming, trying to pull out her own hair. She looked like some cartoon version of a mad professor, plaits yanked out, hair sticking up everywhere. She had her favourite doll in one hand and was bouncing on the bed, screaming ceaselessly and rhythmically whacking her doll's head against the wall. And with some force, as well. I flew towards her.

She went stiff as I grabbed her and, ignoring the stench, wrapped my arms around her as tight as dared to. Then I rocked her, very gently, till little by little, her body loosened and her screams turned first to howls and then to whimpers, before finally subsiding to sobs.

And as I sat there on the bed with her, I took in the devastation. She'd ripped up books and strewn them everywhere, she'd torn down her curtains, and I could see what looked like a puddle of urine on the carpet; it was already seeping into the bottom of my sock. Leaning slightly forward I could also see into the waste-paper basket, where she'd obviously just done another poo. It was smeared all over it, I could see now, both inside and out, and I realised that, in the absence of any paper, she'd used her hands to do it, as well. Further investigation confirmed it. She was covered in smears of faeces. So, I slowly realised, was I.

It must have been a mark of how strangely the human mind works under stress, because my first thought – my only thought – as I sat there and held her was, *Great! Why hadn't she finished it in the bloody neighbour's garden!*

My gentle probing, after the event, long after I'd cleaned her and cuddled her and reassured her she wasn't evil, gleaned nothing. Nothing at all. So all I could do was what I had been doing from Day One. Log it in my journal, for the record.

But it wasn't just Olivia who was giving me cause to worry increasingly about the kids' fragility. Ashton too was regressing very badly. Only a few days later, while Mike and I were dishing up tea, we heard a huge commotion in the back garden. Both kids – I could clearly hear Ashton yelling – and Bob, too, it seemed. He just wouldn't stop barking.

We both flew outside to find the children in a tangle on the muddy grass, while Bob stood nearby, a spectator. They were going at it, fighting like a pair of caged animals, kicking each other, punching each other, pulling out tufts of hair. It took Mike, big as he was, to fully separate them.

I was shocked. I'd never seen them fight like this before. Bicker, yes, throw the odd punch, the odd slap, but not this. 'She's a fucking skirt!' Ashton was yelling, half deranged with anger, his face scarlet. 'She's nothing but a filthy fucking skirt!'

'He called me a frigid bitch!' Olivia screamed back. 'And a hate him! An' a skirt! You heard him, Mike! He said a skirt!'

It was a full fifteen minutes before we had them both calm enough to be sat down at the table to wait for their tea, but, once again, there was nothing to be learned from them by asking. Every question about what they were fighting about so violently was met by a brace of rueful shrugs.

It was only later, when I was tucking Olivia into bed, that I thought I might try one more time.

'What's a skirt, love?' I asked her mildly. 'It really seemed to upset you, Ashton calling you that. What's it mean?'

She pulled a face that confirmed what I'd already suspected. 'He's *horrible*. It means I'm one of Gwandad's whores. So I shud'n be frigid. *Hate* Ash. He's *mean.*'

Aged just seven, I thought. Childhood? What childhood?

Chapter 20

I grew more convinced, with every passing day, that these children had not been regularly abused by only a family member. I felt sure it went deeper, and wider than that. Every time either of them mentioned a relative – particularly 'Gwandad' – I got this uncomfortable knotted feeling in the pit of my stomach. Gut instinct, I guess was what you'd call it.

By the time John arrived for our next meeting with Anna, at the end of February, I was surer than ever that what we were dealing with was a much bigger thing than perhaps had been thought. So I'd prepared. I'd updated all the recent logs for the children, and also refreshed my memory of the disclosures they already made.

'Morning!' he said cheerfully, as he followed me into the dining room. 'Do I smell coffee?'

'What do you think?' I said. 'Help yourself.'

He did so. 'But, seriously,' he went on, as he sipped it, 'I hear you've been having a bit of a difficult time of it just lately.'

'You could say that,' I answered wryly. 'But what else would I expect?' I reminded him of how he'd reassured me, back when we were looking after Justin, that with the end on the horizon, kids routinely played up and regressed. 'Except when these two regress it's a lot more than just swearing and shouting, believe me. It's bodily functions. And in all their grisly glory, as well.'

John winced. 'I understand,' he said.

I wanted to say 'Do you?', but I didn't. How could he know what it was like to live with? So I shouldn't berate him. He was a friend, being supportive, and there was nothing wrong with that.

The doorbell rang anyway, heralding Anna's arrival. Which meant the meeting could get properly under way.

'Come in and join the party!' I said, taking her coat from her and leading her into the dining room. I also noticed, right away, that she didn't smile at my quip. Indeed, she looked just about as serious as I'd seen her at any point since we'd met her. 'Oh, dear,' I said. 'You look very much like a bearer of bad tidings.'

'That's because I am,' she said simply. 'Truth be told.'

I panicked then, slightly. Exactly how bad were these tidings. Had something changed? Had they given up on finding permanent foster carers? I thought about the alternative: leaving us for separate children's homes, and despaired inwardly. But Anna must have noticed my expression.

'Oh, it's not about the little ones,' she reassured me. 'Well, in so far as it doesn't affect them. Not now at least, for which we should all send up a prayer. No, it's the family, and what's been uncovered about them. It doesn't make for edifying reading.'

I poured her a coffee while she emptied her big bag of its contents. There seemed an awful lot of paperwork all of a sudden. 'Honestly, she said, 'it makes me so angry, it really does. There's so much more in the archives that I didn't know about when we started. But, no, it's just drip, drip ... Should have known about all of this before.'

John and I, like-minded, exchanged a surreptitious glance. Boy, we knew more than *anyone* how that felt.

'Oh, dear,' John said, 'that sounds a bit ominous. Do we need to sit and brace ourselves, ready?'

Anna smiled, though without humour, and pulled out a thick manila envelope. 'Twenty years worth of info is what I have here,' she told us. 'After the court case and the allegations from both the aunt and from Ashton, there's been something not dissimilar to an archaeological dig. And our searches,' she went on, 'have led us down all sorts of avenues, deep within the family, the extended family, and even family friends. And it seems social services have had long dealings with a great number of them, going back, as I say, twenty years.'

'To when the kid's mum – Karen, isn't it? – was tiny, then,' said John.

Anna nodded. 'And Karen is key here. There were all sorts of accusations, allegations and investigations, the last of which was when Karen – and this was before she first fell pregnant – confided to a friend when she was 14 that she'd been having sex with her father for a number of years. Her younger sisters too, allegedly.'

'Doesn't surprise me in the least,' I said. 'But, God, it brings you up short to hear this, doesn't it? That this has been going on, right under social services' nose, for generations.'

'Allegedly,' Anna corrected.

'Not in my mind!' I answered.

'But that's the truth of it, and what's on record makes it clear why. It was Karen herself. As you know, she has quite severe learning difficulties, and was always thought of as slow by the local community. And she was also well known for making stuff up, to get attention, and would apparently often come up with fantastical tales. But for some reason, this particular girl's mother believed her. And her father was arrested. But released without charge.'

'What?' John and I both squawked, in unison. 'How did that happen?' John went on. 'Did she withdraw her statement?'

'Anna nodded. 'She returned to the station with her mother – Granddad's then wife – who it seems, made a pretty convincing show of explaining that her little girl really wasn't right in the head, and had said what she'd said only to cover up the fact that she'd actually been having sex with her boyfriend; having let slip that she was having sex, she panicked, apparently, and said it was her dad to protect the boy.'

'Lovely,' I said. 'How the other half live, eh? But that's crap! How could anyone fall for such garbage? It's an allegation of incest, for God's sake!'

'They didn't believe that, surely?' John added.

'Seems they did,' Anna answered. 'Wouldn't today, I don't doubt. But back then ... you have to remember how taboo all this stuff was.'

'And domestic,' agreed John. 'Which made one hell of a difference. Much more likely to be swept under the carpet than these days. You know – allegation withdrawn, least said, soonest mended, what goes on behind closed doors, in the family, and all that.'

'So it's all pretty pointless information, is what you're saying?' I couldn't help but feel despondent. These people lived among us. Had always lived among us. Completely untroubled, or so it seemed, by any outside 'interference'. As untroubled as they were about morality.

'No, not pointless,' Anna said. 'Because this is the 21st century. And all my digging and delving has actually borne fruit.'

I smiled to myself at her choice of metaphors. Fruit of the kind you had to scramble underground for. It seemed apt.

'In what way?' John asked.

'In that it's brought to light the vast extent of it. A bit of joined-up thinking, this stuff being pulled together ... well, in conjunction with the court ruling and, of course, Casey and Mike's evidence, what we have is a clear picture of the whole extended family – and beyond it – systematically abusing over decades. The whole thing, every bit of it, is now with the powers that be in social services – the head honchos – the plan being that, once it's all been properly collated, it will all be handed over to the police.' She turned to me, her expression one of grim determination. 'Don't you worry, Casey. However long it takes – and it might be a while yet – "Gwandad" will have his day in court.'

'Makes my skin crawl,' Mike said, over a late mug of coffee that evening. 'To think how long this has been happening, how many children have been molested. And not a thing has been done about it. It's unbelievable.'

'And it all fits. All those strange adult things Olivia comes out with. God's wrath, walls have ears and that … God, you can almost hear the bastard saying it.'

'Not surprised. He's had enough time to perfect his technique!'

'Those poor children,' I said. 'Prisoners, that's what they've been. Prisoners in the one place little children should be safe. But at least it's over now, and it shed a new light on Karen for me. To think that when she was little – Olivia's age, probably – she was already being regularly raped by her own father. No wonder the poor girl couldn't cut it as a parent! What does something like that *do* to a person's head, do you think?'

We were never going to know that, of course. Could only speculate, grimly. But at least for the kids there was help on the horizon as, a few days later, the promised visit from the psychiatrist took place. And he was well informed. He was the same doctor who'd prepared the court evaluations, both of the children and the parents; in the latter case, competency testing in order that the court would be able to make a judgment about the couple's ability to parent their children.

It was a long, drawn-out process; Ashton was with him for an hour, Olivia for even longer. By the time she skipped out of the lounge, telling me 'Casey, it's your turn! The doctor wants you!', Mike and I had already eaten our tea. 'He's very funny,' she confided. 'He plays games wif you an' evryfink!'

I agreed it would be fun, and took my 'turn'.

His chat to me was as short as the assessments had been long because he couldn't, he explained, tell me anything concrete till he'd studied the results in greater depth. He did corroborate what we knew about the extent of Olivia's learning difficulties, though, on a positive note, remarked that she was fundamentally quite bright.

'So with the right support, the right environment,' he said, 'there's potential for great improvement. It's Ashton's results, however that most intrigue me. As you know, I have analysed his mother at some length, and Ashton's profile, in terms of the nature of his various problems, is almost identical in every way.'

'Well, she is his mother,' I commented.

'Doesn't matter,' he said. 'This sort of result is almost always only found in siblings. If I'd seen this blind,' he said, speaking even more accurately than he realised, 'I'd think the two of them *were* brother and sister!'

I thought then of that poor, damaged little boy, and his heritage. And what *that* did to a person's head, God only knew.

Chapter 21

It wasn't that I wanted to label the children – God knew, I'd seen how being flagged up as having problems could chip away at a vulnerable child's self-esteem. But I felt a weight had lifted from me after the psychiatrist had seen Ashton and Olivia. It not only represented the first step to getting them psychological support; it also meant I'd get more insight into their poor troubled minds. It didn't even matter that they might leave us in a matter of weeks. It was just comforting to know that they would get the right help, at last, from the right people.

Our 'normal' wasn't like most kinds of 'normal' these days, but as much as it could be called that, that's exactly what it felt like in the weeks following the psychiatrist's visit. There were still the day-to-day challenges surrounding toileting and sexual impropriety, but they went off to school each day in mostly sunny spirits, and returned having not – well, as far as I knew, anyway – caused any problems while there.

Indeed, the tone of life settled into such a relaxed and calm pattern that I would catch myself sometimes having to recall the reality that these two were deeply traumatised, badly abused kids, ripped from the only home and loved ones they'd ever known and whose future was not yet at all certain.

But there were two other children in my life who, in the middle of so much upset, I had not had nearly enough time for.

'You'll regret saying that,' observed Riley, on the Saturday before Easter, when I commented how much I'd been missing them. It was gloriously springlike, we'd had no frost in days, and with the sun beckoning, it was almost as if the daffodils beneath my blossom tree were nodding their cheerful heads in agreement. I'd brewed coffee and followed her outside into the garden.

'Not in a million years,' I replied, scooping my newest grandson up for a much needed cuddle. Well, much needed for me. His grizzling soon made it apparent that what *he* most needed was not to be fussed over by nanna, but left alone, in his pram, for a nap.

Riley parked the pram and took her coffee, then shook her head. 'Yes, you will, Mum. I'm finally learning first hand, believe me, why the terrible twos are called exactly that. He runs me ragged most days, little scamp. And I'm soooo tired.'

'Then it's my turn,' I said. 'Or, by the look of it, Bob's!' Our poor mutt. He'd been out on the lawn, having a post-breakfast doze on the patio, but was now the one who was being run ragged, by a distinctly over-excited Levi, who was chasing the poor thing all round the garden.

'Hey, little man, just calm down!' Riley called, to no effect. 'I'm trying to get your little brother off to sleep!'

'Why don't you wheel him inside, love?' I suggested, popping him back in his pram again. 'Wheel him into the dining room. It's nice and quiet in there. He'll soon drop off.'

Poor Riley, I thought, remembering when Kieron was tiny and how she seemed to have the energy of half a dozen kids. So different from when you have your first child, I thought, when you could just grab a chunk of sleep when the baby did. Not so with a two-year-old, for sure!

'So where's Ashton?' Riley asked once she'd come back out into the garden – or rather the conservatory, as she still wanted to be able to keep an ear out.

'Gone to football with Dad,' I said. 'To watch Kieron play. Learning young, you see, that the secret of a happy *male* Saturday is to get out of the house before any babies arrive! So we're all girls together, today –' I put my head round the kitchen door now. 'Eh, Olivia? Looking after the little ones.'

Olivia, who was sitting at the table, colouring, looked up and nodded. Then went back to her endeavours, which she'd been absorbed in for ages. It was one of those books with lots of really intricate abstract patterns inside, which required many felt pens and a lot of concentration. And for all her problems, Olivia *was* bright, and also turning out to be quite the perfectionist. If she went over the lines even once she could get in a complete state, and the picture would be 'ruined' and often the afternoon with it.

So engrossed had she been, in fact, that it never occurred to me that she'd leave the table. It wasn't until Jackson cried out, half an hour or so later, that I realised she was no longer there. Riley and I had been engrossed too, of course, sitting chatting about babies and routines and the exasperating ways of men generally, and we'd both presumed Jackson was asleep.

Even now I didn't connect the two things. Riley looked at her watch and groaned, then got up to go and see to him. 'Obviously not *that* sleepy,' she commented ruefully.

I got up and followed her. Somewhat deprived of my little grandson lately, I was more than happy to take over the rocking and pacing duties that were such a big, tiring part of having a young baby in your life.

It was only the fact that, when we got there, the door to the dining room was shut that made me wonder where Olivia might be. Riley had left it ajar. I remembered her saying so. So that she could hear from the conservatory if he stirred.

Even without my quite knowing why, my heart lurched. And then my brain caught up, flashing up an image that still upset me, of Olivia and how she had to give her dollies their 'internals'. And even as the horrible thought entered my conscious mind, the door was opened by Riley, and there she was before us, crouched in front of Jackson's pram, both of her hands inside his nappy.

She jumped up, red-faced and clearly startled. 'I ain't done nuffing!' she shouted. 'I swear it, Casey, honest! I was just havin' a check to see if he was wet!'

Riley let out a sound that was almost a howl, then leapt forward and grabbed Jackson from his pram. 'Not again!' she barked. 'Christ!' She pulled the baby to her chest, while Olivia just stood there, hands on hips, looking strangely defiant. 'I ain't done nuffing!' she insisted, glaring at Riley.

I felt my heart lurch. I knew all too well what Riley meant. A year back, when accidently scrammed at by an 18-month-old Levi, our last foster child, Sophia, had slapped him, very hard, across the leg. It had been horrible to witness and had upset me for weeks. I kept thinking that I should have seen it coming. Been more observant, because we knew by then just what a sick child she was. Mentally unstable and prone to dramatic bouts of temper, she had lashed out at him before our very eyes.

And now this. And once again I felt mortified. Mortified that my own grandson wasn't safe in my own home. 'Go to your room please, Olivia,' I said evenly and slowly. 'And stay there till I come up to you, okay?'

This seemed to galvanise her. Edging warily past Riley, as if she might get a cuff around the ear, she did as I'd told her, hurrying up the stairs as quick as her little legs would take her, leaving Riley and I alone with Jackson.

Thankfully, he seemed happy enough, gurgling merrily to himself when Riley laid him down on the sofa, so it

seemed there was no apparent damage. But for all that I
didn't doubt Olivia had no intention of hurting him, we
were still shocked, neither of us knowing what to say or
do.

'Mum,' said Riley finally. 'What do you think she was
doing to him? I mean, I know she wasn't doing what she
said she was. And so do you.'

I shook my head. 'I know, love. What can I say? We just
don't *know*. But I don't think for a minute that she meant
to hurt him.'

'Just have a quick fiddle, then, was that it?' Riley's
accompanying look was withering.

This is how it starts, I thought. *This is how it starts*. This
would have been the sort of thing that happened to Olivia
and all her siblings. Regularly. Unashamedly. Normalising
everything. Making the unspeakable routine. Making a
child's private body parts public property within the family.
So that as they grew they knew no different and so it carried
on. And then, one day, those same children would hit
puberty. Have sexual feelings. And by then, of course, the
damage would have already long been done. It made me
shudder.

Riley reached for her bag of baby paraphernalia, which
was hanging from the handle of the pram. 'I might as well
change him now we're here,' she said, carefully unfastening
his nappy. 'Could you do me a favour and check on Levi for
me, Mum?' She looked up and smiled; a smile designed to
make me feel better. 'Just be sure poor old Bob is surviving
under the stress?'

I nodded. 'And I'll pop up to Olivia as well,' I said. 'Strike, as they say, while the iron's hot.'

What I didn't say, as Riley hadn't been privy to the extent of it, was that I was worried this episode could soon cause another. And another bout of self-abuse, not to mention scrawling on her walls and defecating in her rubbish bin, was exactly what none of us needed today.

But when I got upstairs, Olivia was merely in hiding. She was hiding in her bed, huddled in the corner by the wall, beneath the duvet. I pulled back the covers and sat down, noticing but not mentioning the large wet stain that had spread across both her jeans and the bottom sheet.

'Sweetheart,' I said gently, 'I need you to tell me what it was that you were doing. Now I know that little girls sometimes need to know what their dollies – their baby dollies, especially – have in their nappies. They need to know that, so they can change them, if they're wet. But *was* it that, love? I need you to tell me the truth. Were you *really* checking to see if Jackson had had a pee pee?'

I waited while she seemed to wrestle with her emotions. And then slowly, almost imperceptibly, she shook her head. She started to cry then, and I pulled her close to me, feeling an unexpected wave of tenderness for her, despite what had happened. It wasn't her fault, for God's sake; it was the fault of those bloody monsters. She didn't know why she had done it, did she? How could she? If you asked her to explain, on pain of death, why she'd been rooting in his nappy, the poor mite wouldn't be able to tell you in a million years. It was just what she'd seen and had done to her all her life. It was normal. 'Family' life. It made my blood boil.

But there was hope too, I realised, in all this. She was beginning to realise it was *wrong*. That it was not at all normal. That it upset people.

'Riley hates me now, don't she?' she mumbled into my jumper.

'No, love,' I said. 'Not at all. She doesn't hate you. But she's a mummy, and you know what it's like to be a mummy, don't you? They get upset when they think someone might have harmed their baby.'

She pulled back so she could look at me, 'I wasn't hurting him! I *swear*! I was just 'aving a feel. Just a tickle, that's all.'

It was at that moment when Riley herself appeared in the bedroom doorway, holding Jackson. 'Olivia,' she said, without anger or malice. 'You are seven years old. A big girl now. And I know you've been told all about good touching and bad touching, haven't you? And that was bad touching, wasn't it? You know that. And that's why you're feeling so bad at this moment. Because you *know*.' She let this sink in a moment, never taking her eyes off Olivia, then said, 'So what I want you to promise me is that you will never do that again. Can you do that?'

Olivia looked stricken, unable to answer. Then pushed her face into the wool of my jumper once again, crying, 'I'm sorry, Riley! I'll kill myself if you want. I really will!'

'Olivia,' said Riley,' that's the *last* thing I want. All I want is for you to promise me, that's all.'

I stroked Olivia's hair. 'You can do that, love, can't you?' I whispered.

'I pwomise,' she mumbled, between sobs.

For all that it pretty much put the lid on our carefree Saturday, when the evening came and I sat down to write up the incident, it occurred to me again there had been progress made here. For the first time I had a clear sense that not only did Olivia know she'd done something to make the grown-ups cross, but actually had a real sense of *why*. Riley's words had been spot-on. It was the fact that Olivia knew she'd done wrong that had caused her so much upset and self-loathing. It was a horrible process for her to have to live through and learn from, but learn she must. Her whole psyche essentially had to be recalibrated; she had to reject the norms of her early childhood – already hard-wired into her – and replace them with the morals of the society in which we lived. Such a very big thing for such a very little girl. But it was necessary; the alternative prospect was so much worse. Abused children often only realise that they're being abused once their own sex hormones, and greater knowledge of their abuser's sick motivation, begin to kick in. And, as countless tragic testimonies prove, by that time the damage runs horribly deep.

Even so, it was frustrating when things like this happened. Why couldn't progress with these kids be more linear? We'd make some, then just when I thought we were winning, there'd be a reminder that there was still such a long, long way to go. I was fretting more, with each passing week, about their potential new placements. The kids needed to be seen as manageable prospects. We'd seen it all before, of course; our remit was to foster the 'unfosterable', but the vast majority of foster carers neither wanted, nor were experienced in handling, such challenging kids.

'You're wrong,' said Mike, bringing me a welcome dose of caffeine. 'The trouble is, you can't see the wood for the trees. You've worked miracles. You've worked magic. You're just too close to it to see it. You've taken two broken kids and you're slowly but surely putting them back together. So stop beating yourself up, love, okay. You're doing *brilliantly*.'

It didn't feel that way to me, but as words went, they were pretty nice, and very timely ones. And that was all we *could* do, really. Just keep on doing what we were doing. Just teaching these poor mites how to live, basically, before we had to let them go, all the while crossing our fingers behind our backs.

Chapter 22

Just as had happened at Christmas, Easter passed almost unnoticed by the children. Though Mike and I did our usual mammoth Easter egg hunt – planting scores of brightly wrapped Easter eggs all around the garden – it was, perhaps predictably, only our big kids, plus little Levi, who fully engaged with the process.

'I can't believe it!' I said to Mike as we stood in the conservatory doorway, watching our two grown-up children, plus little Levi, dashing from bush to bush, possessed. 'Look at those two, will you? Twenty and twenty-two, going on eight or nine. And then those two –' here I pointed towards Olivia and Ashton, who both had a look of faint bewilderment. 'Doesn't matter how much grim information we hear about the family from social services, I still can't get my head round the fact that this is all so alien to them! I mean, surely they must have been in supermarkets

257

around Easter time. Surely they watched telly. Surely they made Easter cards at school!'

Mike shook his head. 'You know, Case, the more I think about it, the more I think you were right in what you said the other day. Yes, they went to school, but as for the rest, I think that's just it. I wonder if perhaps they really *were* prisoners in their own home. I mean, if you are systematically abusing all the children in the family, then the last thing you'd want is them out of your sight, mixing with other people, perhaps letting things slip. Far better to keep them in, I'd say, wouldn't you?'

I watched Ashton and Olivia, trying their best to join in. Tragically, I suspected Mike was right.

But the past was done and dusted and as the summer term got under way, I felt the longer days and welcome sunshine helped me focus on the here and now, and when I received a call from Dr Shackleton, telling me he'd got the reports back from the psychiatrist, I felt a renewed sense of sleeves-up, can-do.

I made an appointment to go down and discuss them with them the following day and no sooner had I disconnected than the phone rang again. This time in was Anna, and she was about to rock my world.

'Hi,' she said brightly. 'I've got some really great news!'

'Well, that would certainly make a pleasant change,' I said, wondering what it might be. 'What is it?

'We think we've found some carers to take Olivia!'

It was as if I'd had a stone dropped from a great height, into my stomach. I was gutted. And what's more, I felt shocked that I was so gutted. All this time I'd spent badgering social services about placements, and now Anna had come good, it had hit me so hard. I was silent for some seconds. It was actually hard to catch my breath.

'Are you sure?' I said eventually. Was I hoping she'd say, 'Actually, no, it was just a joke'?

'Well, obviously not quite sure,' she chattered on happily. 'Nothing will be concrete till they've met her, as you know. And of course first I'll have to visit you, so I can tell you all about them, and then Olivia will have to meet them, and ... Casey, is something wrong? You don't sound very happy. I thought you'd be jumping for joy!'

I'd grown quite fond of Anna, as it happened. Our professional relationship should have lasted only a few weeks, but as things had worked out, almost nine months had passed now, and in that time, though it was sometimes exasperating dealing with social services, I'd come to trust that she was as committed to these little ones as we were; that they weren't just one caseload in a file among many. That she was emotionally engaged with Olivia and Ashton. And that she understood just how much I was. So her breezy comment brought me up short. Like it was really that simple? That I could simply disengage? Just like that?

But that was unfair of me. Anna's job was wholly differ-ent to mine and Mike's one. Her job was to remain detached – well, to a fair degree, anyway. Her job was to objectively assess the circumstances of the families she came into contact with, then take action in the best interests of the child or children. Her job was then to place them. Not to live with them or to care for them. Just move them along the care system; every bit as important a job as mine or any other foster carer's. And she was young. Not yet a parent. How could she possibly understand that depth of maternal feeling? How could she appreciate the love you can't help but feel?

No, it wasn't fair to judge her. She sounded happy because she was happy and, in time, I would be too. The best interests of the children involved them being placed in secure settled homes, far away from the ravages of their former childhoods.

'Yes, of course I'm pleased,' I said. 'It's just knocked me for six a bit. You know, all this time waiting and now it's finally happened, all I can think about is how much I'll miss her and all her funny little ways.'

'Oh, bless,' Anna said, soothingly. 'It must be hard, letting them go. I don't know how you do it, I really don't.'

Which seemed the right place to draw a line under that particular conversation. We let them go because that's what we'd chosen to do. I'd been here before, with Justin, and had spent many, many sleepless nights wondering if we should keep him. But that had never been my intention when I'd signed up to become a specialist carer. I'd signed up because I believed passionately that I could help *lots* of children. Take the older kids, the kids who were the most deeply troubled and unloved, and then send them on their way, hopefully fixed up sufficiently that they had had a chance of a happy adult life.

I said to myself out loud: 'Casey, get a grip on yourself. You should have expected to feel like this at this point, you silly woman.'

It's one thing to tell yourself you're being silly, of course, but quite another to stop the feelings coming. And I knew it was a time thing. If Ashton and Olivia had been placed within the few weeks we'd been promised, of course I wouldn't be in bits like this. At that point, it was fair to say, I would have been relieved. They had been a nightmare to live with in the early days, by anyone's yardstick, and it was only our sense of professional responsibility (and, let's face it, who else would have them?) that had stopped Mike and I demanding they be moved.

But these kids had been a huge part of my life for almost a year now. We'd barely been parted. It was like when my own two were that age – you live kids and breathe kids, mould your lifestyle around them, and though they weren't my kids I had truly grown to love them. So, yes, this was going to be hard.

'C'mon, love, pipe down,' Mike whispered in the early hours of the next morning, after I'd lain awake sobbing, unable to find sleep. I'd fixated on another heartbreaking thought, as the day had gone on. Ashton. Poor, poor Ashton. How was he going to cope seeing his sister taken away, and with the realisation that no-one wanted him? Because Anna had been clear. There was nothing on the horizon. Always the way. He was older, which just made everything that bit harder, and he was also a boy, which made it harder still. Prejudice against boys – the idea that they were generally much more challenging to look after than girls – never really seemed to go away.

And we hadn't even told the kids they were to be separated yet. The thought of doing that – even though I knew it was the right thing – filled me with something approaching dread.

'I'm sorry, love,' I sniffed, 'I just can't seem to help it. I just can't stop thinking about poor Ashton. How will he cope?'

'But you must,' Mike answered, his voice still low but his tone firm. 'If the kids hear you crying they're going to get in a right state, which will just make the whole thing much worse. It'll work out. You know it will. And you've got to toughen up. It'll be weeks before Olivia goes, the pace these things move at, and if you're all doom and gloom and crying it will mess with their heads.'

'I know, I do know that. And I will do, I promise. I just needed a bit of a cry, that's all.'

He held me tighter. 'And you've certainly had it,' he said. 'Look! My bloody pillow's completely soaked!'

The bout of sobbing obviously helped, because when I woke the next morning I felt one hundred per cent better. And with my default disposition of cheerful optimism restored, which was a blessing, I could begin to tot up all the positives in my head.

First stop was the appointment I'd arranged with Dr Shackleton, who ran through a whole range of psychological stuff with me, some of it just a little bit beyond my comprehension, but that didn't matter. That was for whichever professional counsellors were put in place, once the kids were settled in their new lives.

From my point of view, however, the most important thing was that Olivia had been also diagnosed as dyspraxic. Dyspraxia, though related, was different from dyslexia, and right away, as Dr Shackleton ran through the range of symptoms, I could recognise so much in Olivia. It was almost, in fact, as if the list had been specially made to describe her. *At last*, I thought, *something we can put a name to.*

'Of course, this has implications for school,' Dr Shackleton explained. 'You'll obviously have a home visit from the occupational therapist, and she'll then liaise directly with Olivia's current primary school; make sure they know what they're dealing with and support her accordingly.'

Though she'd not be at her primary for much longer, it seemed. Not if everything went well with her potential new carers.

Not that my positive mood stopped me from eyeing them up like a sulky teenager when I watched the car that contained them, driven by Anna, pull up outside our house the following Monday.

But my fears were swept away in an instant.

Called Mick and Sandie, they were a sweet childless couple in their forties, who lived about thirty miles away.

They'd already been carers for fifteen years, and seemed to have a great deal to offer. They seemed relaxed, energetic and, best of all by far, lived on a farm, with horses and livestock. I could so easily visualise the sort of life Olivia could have with them, and an Enid Blyton picture fixed itself pleasingly in my mind. Lashing of lemonade, climbing trees, making daisy chains, learning to ride. All in all, it felt almost too good to be true.

Which meant it was hugely important that I spell everything out for them. Too many placements broke down, and I'd seen it, because carers plunge in without knowing the full facts. It was understandable; with so much pressure on social services to find homes for children, they couldn't be blamed for painting a slightly rosy picture, could they? Even if unconsciously. But this was not going to be like that in this case. I was determined. They had to know exactly what sort of child they'd be taking on.

All this was going through my mind as I bustled around making coffee, aware of Anna chatting to them and them commenting on all Olivia's pictures, which by now dominated not only the front of the fridge freezer, but much of the kitchen wall space, as well.

I brought the coffee to the table. She loves her colouring,' I told them. 'She quite artistic, as you can see. And such a lovely little girl. I'm really going to miss her.'

They nodded politely, accepting coffees. Mick, tall and ruddy, looked every inch the man who lived an outdoor life, and Sandie, reed thin, was very smiley, and capable-looking. I felt sure Olivia would be in good hands. Sandie was blonde, too, with hair not dissimilar to Olivia's. Of no consequence whatsoever – slightly bonkers, in fact – but the visual 'fit' in itself reassured me.

'But,' I said, after I'd run through my mentally prepared long list of positives, 'there are challenges, which you need to be aware of.' I spotted Anna stiffening as I said this, but ignored her. 'She wets her bed regularly,' I said. 'Sometimes wets herself during the day, too.'

Sandie smiled at me. 'Been there, done that!' She said brightly. 'Had one little one nearly finished off my washing machine for me. I was laundering sheets morning, noon and night!'

'And she also soils,' I said. 'Not often now, thankfully, but it's still a problem. Particularly if she's badly stressed or upset.' I took a breath. 'And it's not always just in her pants.' I went on to explain that it was an emotional response, and, as such, could involve soiling in unlikely places. I mentioned the bin in her bedroom, and watched them blanch. But they rallied.

Mick said, 'But it sounds as if you've made lots of progress with her, though. From what Anna was telling me in the car – and from the profile we've read – she was almost feral when you got her, wasn't she?'

I nodded. 'There's been an amazing amount of progress,' Anna confirmed, 'with both the children. Such a turn-around ...'

'Though there's still a way to go,' I said firmly. 'As you'll know from the files, it's probable that Olivia has been groomed – sexually abused – perhaps from babyhood. So

265

there is still a strong tendency for her to lapse into deviant behaviours, less so now, as Anna says, but as I'm sure you both know, these sorts of things can't just be magicked away.'

'Though CAMHS will obviously be involved in that side of things,' Anna added. 'She'll be having regular counselling put in place right away.'

I continued: 'She also has obsessions. They come and go, but they also reflect her traumatic early life. Death and disaster. Fire. Things like that.'

'Well,' said Mick, 'there's certainly a lot to think about, isn't there?' He looked at his wife, who nodded agreement, but there was something in her expression which reassured me that she *was* thinking; and not just, 'Oh my God – nightmare!'

And so they went away and thought. And the wait to hear from them, as the week crawled by, was beginning to seem interminable. Though Anna hadn't said as much, I knew she was thinking I had only myself to blame if they called and said they'd changed their minds. I so wanted them to meet Olivia. That couldn't happen till they were fairly sure, of course – too disrupting and potentially upsetting for her – but still I stood by my reasoning that it *had* to be this way. Much as I couldn't bear the thought of saying goodbye to her, it would be so much more painful to send her off on her new journey, only to have it all fall apart.

And I would *so* miss her. Impressively, the new learning support had already been put in place at school, and she was as bouncy and excited about it all as I'd ever seen her.

'God, Livs, do you ever shut up?' grumbled Ashton as we ambled back from school the following Tuesday.

'Shut up yourself, Ash,' she rebuked him, barely pausing for breath as she continued regaling me with all the things she'd done in school today. It took me right back – to the differences between boys and girls, in terms of how much they had to say. It had been exactly the same with my two. Monosyllabic grunts from Kieron – 'Do I *have* to tell you what I did, Mum?' – and a non-stop stream of gossip from my daughter. Nothing had changed.

'And I got moved for maffs!' Olivia chirruped. 'And I get special treatment an' everyfing! I got tooked out! By a special teacher. And she sat and helped me learn it. An' it was good. She said it would stop me getting in such a kerfluffle.'

'Kerfuffle,' I corrected, laughing.

'Ker – *fuff* – le!' Ashton echoed.

'No, she definitely said kerfluffle. What is a kerfluffle anyway? Well, whatever it is, I was definitely doin' it.' She grinned up at me. 'An' now I'm not!'

I pulled both the kids in for an impromptu bear hug. I could have eaten them up right there on the spot.

Chapter 23

The call came from Anna just over a week later.

'Right, we're on,' she said. 'Well, to the next stage, at least.'

'Oh, that's brilliant,' I said, feeling a profound sense of relief. Though I was dreading the day we said goodbye and I lost Olivia, I wouldn't have forgiven myself if my enthusiasm to paint an uncompromisingly realistic picture had sent Mick and Sandie running scared and pulling out.

'I know,' she agreed. 'Fabulous news, isn't it? And they're keen to crack on, so how are you fixed for this coming Saturday?' *Strike while the iron's hot*, I thought. 'You free?'

'Absolutely,' I said. 'I'll just have to see if Riley can have Ashton.'

'No, bring him along. They're fine with that. I explained the circumstances to them, and I think it would arouse less suspicion if you did it that way.'

'And who knows?' I said, a flicker of hope igniting inside me. 'Perhaps they'll take to him so much that they'll want him as well!'

Anna was quiet for a moment, and rightly so. I knew the facts, didn't I? The kids were being separated primarily for their own good. Stupid woman, I berated myself. What was I *saying*?

'Ignore me,' I said, before she had a chance to remind me. 'Wishful thinking, that's all. On which note, any developments in that direction yet?'

I heard a sigh. 'I'm afraid not,' she said.

The plan was that Mike and I would explain away the visit to Mick and Sandie's as being just one of those things foster carers did. We'd be going to visit them to find out more about them, discuss foster-caring-type issues and (since the visit was as much about getting Olivia familiar with the surroundings) have a good look around their house. It was generally done this way – or a version of it, anyway – because there was no guarantee, even with all the information in the world, that a carer or carers would 'click' with a child, and for that child to go through the process of being 'sized up' a number of times would be potentially very damaging psychologically.

And, incredible though it seemed, they swallowed what we told them, perhaps because they had so little normal life-experience anyway that they took pretty much everything they were told at face value.

And without any agenda, or reason to feel anxious, the

two of them, as we set off, on a cloudless summer morning, behaved very much as normal from the off.

'So do you fink you might live on a farm next?' asked Olivia, as we left the city behind and headed off into the green of the countryside.

'Well, you never know,' answered Mike. 'It's nice in the countryside. Lots of space and fresh air for children to run around in, and –'

'Lots of smells!' remarked Ashton, who had opened his window and taken in a lungful of the classic rural odour of silage, or muck-spreading, or both. 'Euww!' he said, grimacing across at Mike. 'That's gross!'

As Ashton had always suffered a little bit with car sickness, I'd allowed him to ride in the front seat for the trip, while I sat in the back, with Olivia. 'An' animals!' she was saying now, excitedly. 'I *love* animals. When I'm growed up, I'm gonna have a pony.'

'Mick and Sandie, who we're visiting,' I told her, 'have ponies. And horses. And cows, too, and sheep.'

'They got sheeps, Pol! Baaa!' Olivia told her dolly, holding her up so she could look out of the car window better at the backdrop of fields and trees and hedgerows speeding by. I glanced across at her, hair freshly washed, pretty dress on, full of smiles. How could they not love her? I discreetly crossed my fingers, even so.

But I was glad, all the same, that I'd prepared the ground so carefully, because within minutes of our arrival, in what seemed almost like a test, Olivia, over-excited on seeing a real-life pony in Mick and Sandie's farmyard, wet herself. And right away I got a good feeling about the prospect of this placement happening, because Sandie's response was as warm as it was instant.

'Oh, don't you worry, sweetheart,' she told Olivia, who was standing in the puddle she'd created, going beetroot. 'Toffee here has little accidents all the time, don't you, Toffee?' She stroked the pony's nose, then leaned down to whisper to Olivia. 'And when a pony has a pee, you know all about it. Soaked my jeans right through last week, he did!'

I'd bought a change of clothing, of course. I tended to do it automatically. And when I took Olivia inside to help her change, my gut feeling was further strengthened. The place was full of photographs of children; many, many different children, too. There were also pictures that had obviously been lovingly painted by children, and a mish-mash of objects on various horizontal surfaces that had clearly been made by children, too. Here a handmade Easter card, there a horse fashioned out of modelling clay; the whole farmhouse was a treasure trove of artefacts and memories, and even though my first thought was, predict-ably, about the dusting, my second was that the whole place just felt right.

Not that Ashton, unlike his sister, agreed with me.

'That man smells of poo,' he whispered to me, wrinkling his nose up, as Mick showed us around the farm. I didn't have much experience of farms and all things rural, but it seemed to me that Mick and Sandie's was a nice one. As well as the stables, where they gave riding lessons to local children, they had a field full of sheep and another one, of cattle, and all sorts of fowl – I spotted hens immediately, and different kinds of geese, all of which were running free around the farmyard. To my untutored eye, bathed in sunshine, it looked idyllic.

'It's not him,' I whispered back. 'It's just his boots, I expect.'

'Well, whatever it is, it stinks,' he said, singularly unimpressed.

But if I was secretly rather pleased to discover Ashton's newly acquired sensibilities regarding matters of hygiene, it was clear he had no interest in the visit. I wondered to myself, 'Does he know something? Has he twigged something's happening? Has he noticed Mick and Sandie's engagement with Olivia?' Not that there was any point where this had been overt. They had tried to include him too, as we sat and chatted about their lives there, but he seemed intent on disengaging and spent the remainder of the visit sitting on a window seat, staring out of the window.

But both kids, to my great joy, had behaved politely and well, and I couldn't have been more pleased if they had been my own.

And Sandie had obviously been impressed too. 'You must be so proud of them,' she said, squeezing my arm as we were leaving. 'From everything we've read, and, well, what you've told us – well, I can scarcely believe they are the same children, can you?'

And when I thought about it, I couldn't.

Even so, the two days between the visit and Anna's next call seemed interminable. Having glimpsed the life Olivia could have if Mick and Sandie agreed to have her, it was grim to contemplate the prospect of them deciding against.

My relief was huge, then, when Anna called and confirmed what I'd hoped for; that Mick and Sandie had agreed to become Olivia's new carers, and even better, they wanted to keep her permanently. This was the best news imaginable and I was so thrilled I whooped, only to be brought down to earth moments later.

'So I think it's probably time for us to sit the children down and tell them what's happening,' Anna added. 'Which I'll be happy to come up and do, of course.'

Again, this was the usual protocol. When a child leaves a foster family, the normal course of action is for the social worker to be the one to break the news to them – *not* the current carers. This is because they need to support the child through the transition and this isn't an easy thing to do if the child thinks their current foster family are a part of the decision-making process. *We love you*, in bald terms, *but not enough to want to keep you*. Better for a white lie to be deployed in this regard than to further damage a child's sense of worth.

But, whoever was going to do the telling in this case, I felt strongly that now wasn't the right time. And said so. 'I just feel we should hold off for the moment,' I explained to Anna. 'As it stands, there's a home for Olivia, but nowhere for Ashton, and all the while we can hold off, I think we should.'

'But they need to know,' Anna answered quietly but firmly. 'So they can prepare themselves. I know it's going to be tough, Casey, but we can't hold off for ever. And it'll be me doing the telling, so it's not as if –'

'It's not about who *does* it. It's about Ashton and what it might *do* to him. It's going to be bad enough for him, knowing he's going to be split up from his sister, let alone knowing she's sorted but no-one wants to take him. I just think we should leave it till the last possible moment. Give it as long as possible. Please?'

Anna agreed, albeit grudgingly, because to her mind it was pointless. With nothing on the horizon till the next round of the panel, she felt it would be worse to keep things stringing along. Mick and Sandie were ready to take Olivia whenever we were and, to Anna's mind, the sooner the kids knew what was happening, the longer they would have to prepare for it. But as it turned out, my plea for more time had been a sound one, because within the week she'd called back; there was finally good news. Another couple, Kerry and Ian, who were in their thirties and lived just ten miles away, had expressed interest in taking on Ashton.

It really was as if God had decided to answer my un-spoken prayer. They'd been unavailable, as they'd been fostering a similarly aged boy long term, but, quite out of the blue, an aunt, previously working abroad, had returned to the UK and said she'd have him. It had been a lengthy process to arrange it and, until agreed, it hadn't been certain, hence no mention of them having been made up till now, in case the handover had all fallen through.

But it hadn't, and they now had a boy-shaped hole in their lives. And like Mick and Sandie, they were very experienced carers.

So, once again, two weeks later, we were back on the road, visiting another foster family to 'see their house'.

'You know,' observed Olivia, once again in the back with me, for another, albeit this time shorter, journey. 'Don't you fink you're being a bit nosy? Mike, you should tell her –' she looked at Mike now, through the rear-view mirror. 'It's rude to go snoopin' around other people's houses, jus' so you can see what stuff they got there.'

Conscious of Ashton's lack of engagement at Mick and Sandie's, I made a big effort this time to get him interested and engage him, as did Ian, who kept dragging him off while we chatted, to get to know the dog, take a look at the garden and even to chat to the gaggle of young boys who had been out playing on the street when we'd arrived and who obviously knew the couple – and their previous lad – well.

And our intention obviously didn't go unnoticed. 'Mike,' Ashton asked, as we made the short journey home, 'those people want to foster us, don't they?'

Mike's eyes immediately met mine, again though the rear-view mirror, and within a second I watched them move to Olivia.

I turned to face her. She looked stricken, and for a moment I was dumbstruck. Unprepared for the conversation we were now obviously going to have. I took her hand, but at the same time, I mostly addressed Ashton. He'd turned around to face me now and his expression was questioning. 'Well,' I said carefully, 'now, there's a thought, actually. They *are* foster carers, and they don't currently have kids in. Why?' I added lightly. 'Did you like them, Ashton?'

Ashton glanced at Olivia, who was clearly waiting for his answer. Then he shrugged. 'Ian was pretty cool, I guess.'

I turned to Olivia, as Ashton swivelled back to face forwards. 'Well, then,' I said brightly, 'we shall see, then.'

And that was how we left it, by what seemed like an unspoken contract. I didn't mention it again, and neither did either of the children. It was almost as if they were two little frightened toddlers, all of a sudden. If they put their hands over their eyes, then they couldn't see anything. And if you couldn't see something, then, naturally, it didn't exist.

The wait this time, happily, was equally short. Within just three days, Ian and Kerry had got in touch with social services and confirmed that they'd like to take on Ashton.

'Incredible, isn't it?' I told Mike when he got home that evening. 'All this time waiting and the two of them were there, perfect for Ashton, all along. Just needed to be free so they could take him, and now they are. It was all meant to be, don't you think?'

I handed him a coffee. 'Thanks, love. Who knows?' he said, sipping it. 'I'm just glad it's not hanging over us any more.' He frowned then. 'But I'm guessing tonight's the night, then, is it?'

I nodded. 'Anna's coming after tea. Around eight. I'm dreading it.'

He grimaced. 'Me too, love. So what's the plan? What's she going to tell them, exactly? We'll need to know if we're going to go along with it, won't we?'

'There doesn't seem to be much of one, to be honest,' I told him. 'She's just going to tell them that's how the rules work. I did ask her how she'd explain it – I mean, siblings do get fostered together all the time; that's what I said to her. I mean, look at these two, and their younger siblings … But, now I've thought about it, I'm beginning to see the sense in it. After all, if you make up all sorts of nonsense to explain it, then you have to keep it up, justify it, don't you? At least this way, we can just go in and present them with a *fait accompli*. Tell them it's just the rules. We can't change them. End of story.'

Mike was still frowning, his forehead etched with grooves you could hold a five pence piece in. 'God, it's just so bloody grim, though, so bloody wretched that it has to be this way.'

I knew how he felt. I'd spent so many hours lying awake wishing it could be different. But it couldn't, and I think I finally understood that now. However much the sexual behaviour had diminished since we'd had them, keeping Ashton with Olivia, especially as they approached adolescence, would be like locking a heroin addict in a room with a loaded syringe. Well, maybe it wasn't quite as stark a scenario as that. But even so, it was definitely not in either child's best interests. They clearly loved one another, and away from the world's rules, who was to say that they wouldn't find physical comfort in one another, and in a way that had seemed so normal as to be mundane for so long?

In the event, it was something of an anticlimax. Which I perhaps should have anticipated, now I knew the children as I did. They both knew they were moving on, so this was just the confirmation. And, as with Christmas and Easter, and anything else outside their experience, they simply responded by digesting it, then seemingly forgetting all about it. I knew this wasn't all there was to it. That when the day came it would be *awful*. But once Anna left, they had only two questions.

'So will we still see you an' Mike and baby Levi, then?' was Olivia's.

'Of course!' I said, cuddling her tiny frame. 'Definitely! Goodness me, I don't think I could bear to part with you if you couldn't both come back to visit us!'

Upon which she patted me, much as she patted her dollies. 'Aww, Casey,' she soothed. 'You'll be *fine*.'

Ashton's was equally direct. 'Together?' he wanted to know, his face serious. 'I mean, will we be allowed to see each other?' he finished, taking in what I'd just said to his sister.

'Yes, definitely,' I said, before I could stop the words coming. Which for all I knew, and I cursed myself crossly for not checking, might have been the one thing I didn't want to tell either of them. A lie.

Chapter 24

It was agreed that we'd say goodbye to the children in two stages. Ashton would go to Ian and Kerry's on the Saturday and Olivia to Mick and Sandie's on the Sunday; a weekend I would not be forgetting in a while.

The remaining four weeks passed in a blur. It had been agreed that the best thing, in terms of least disruption, would be for the children to see the academic year out in school. That way they could spend the summer holidays getting settled, before the upheaval of moving into new – and different – primary schools. And it was as if the initial shock and trauma now over with, we'd all, individually, made a decision to put the whole thing out of our minds. We sorted nothing, packed nothing, made no arrangements. And though both children had been on further visits, this time without us, we all just carried on – unbelievably – as if none of it was happening.

Well, almost. The children, shortly after being told, had been sent parcels. Both sets of new foster carers, just as we did for our kids, had put together portfolios, telling the children all about their families, so they could get to know them all a little better. They also spent time answering the questionnaires the new carers sent them. What did they most like doing? What did they not? Did they have any favourite foods? Things that made them go 'yuk'?. Did they have any TV programmes they particularly liked watching? Were there any special toys they'd be bringing along?

The children seemed to enjoy this process greatly, and it occurred to me that all of us like answering questions about ourselves; it is a way of the telling the world who you are, that you are an individual. That you were special and – crucially – that you mattered.

We also spent time making memory boxes, Riley, as ever, deploying her talents in all matters cutting and sticking related.

'Mine needs to be glittery,' Olivia told her, one morning in July, a couple of weeks before the big day was happening. 'Glittery and pink, like my bedroom. D'you fink Mick an' Sandie will gimme a pink bedroom?'

Riley glanced at me. I nodded. ''Course they will,' I said. 'Because that's what you asked for when you wrote to them, wasn't it? In fact,' I said, riffling through our big pile of craft paper. 'I bet they're painting it pink right this *minute*.'

Ashton, across the table, was similarly employed. Riley had found two robust boxes for the children, both from shoe shops, and which had previously housed boots. We'd already covered his in a layer of denim-effect sticky-backed plastic, and he was busy finding things with which to decorate it.

'What about you, Ash?' Riley asked him. 'What are you going to do with your one?'

He glanced up at her. He was filling out now; he'd be 11 in the autumn, and I could already see the features of a handsome young man. 'I'm gonna make it like a pair of jeans, with badges on,' he said, pulling pictures from the pile in front of him. I'd spent a good hour copying photographs for the kids to use as decoration, as well as giving them free rein with my over-stuffed arts and crafts box.

But it was what went in the boxes that was the primary concern. All children in care are encouraged to make memory boxes. With some poor kids moving several times over the period of their childhood, the aim of having a box of things to take with them was to give them a sense of childhood that otherwise might be lacking. A pictorial history of good times – it was relentlessly about good times – it would hopefully go some way towards balancing the bad times that were obviously a big part of these kids' lives. Thinking about the box made by Justin could still bring a lump to my throat, even now. By the time he'd come to us, he'd been the veteran of twenty failed placements; he'd been from foster home to children's home and back – a proper boomerang. By the time we saw it, the box – and its contents – looked every bit as travelled as if Phileas Fogg had done his romp around the world with it.

But for these two – their only experience of the care system with us – we had the privilege of creating their boxes alongside them. And these boxes (and I mentally kept crossing my fingers) would begin here and end their journey at Mick and Sandie's, Ian and Kerry's. No, it wasn't certain – placements failed. It was a fact we had to live with. But if my positive mental attitude could have any influence over anything, I fervently hoped it was focussed on that.

It was the two boxes that first caught my eye on that Saturday morning. Once they'd been made, and had dried, we'd all set about filling them; a proper family occasion, on Sunday a couple of weeks back, after tea. I'd specifically asked the kids to come over and help us, so the dining-room table had been jam-packed. Kieron and Lauren had come over, as had Riley and David, and Levi and Jackson. Kieron had even dressed a very patient Bob up in some goofy outfits, just so he could take some mad photos of him, upload them on our laptop, then print out copies to go in the kids' boxes then and there.

And I'd not been idle, either. Ever mindful of our role in these children's futures, there'd hardly been a moment where I'd not had it in mind. So I'd kept all sorts of things to remind them of our adventures. Some pretty shells they'd gathered on our Welsh seaside holiday; some shards of driftwood, a couple of particularly pretty pebbles … though I'd passed on the opportunity to slip in any pictures of the Teletubbies' party in Ashton's box.

As I took them down for where we'd put them for safe-keeping – the top of the fridge-freezer – I felt tears smart in my eyes. I'd popped in a couple of other bits and bobs for them, too. For Olivia a brand new set of doll's clothes for the current favourite 'Polly', which I'd secretly had my mother knit for me, and for Ashton three special Dinky cars: two vintage, as a reminder of his time with Mike at the car rally, and, even better, a model of our own car. I'd also popped in some chocolate coins for them both, and DVDs of two kids' films they'd loved. None of these were strictly memory box items, and probably wouldn't stay there, but I'd wanted to give each of them a couple of small gifts without the emotional stress involved in actually presenting them. They could find them later, on their own. That felt best.

I felt rather than heard Mike come into the kitchen. His arm snaked around me as he spoke into my ear. 'Anna's here, love,' he said. 'Stiff upper lip and all that.'

She was in the kitchen with us moments later, and I found myself grateful that she was her normal breezy self. Perhaps she realised that any display of sympathy today would cause a crack in my carefully constructed carapace.

And it was important that I keep it together for Ashton, who had spent the last evening, as together we packed the suitcase with his clothes, doing a sterling job of doing just that. I knew it was important that I didn't let him down.

'So,' Anna asked, 'all packed and ready to roll?' I glanced out through the kitchen door to the back garden, where Ashton and Olivia were playing with Bob.

'You sure you don't want to stop and have a coffee?' I asked her.

She shook her head. 'Better if we crack on,' she said firmly. 'Lovely day for it, anyway,' she added, clapping her hands together cheerfully. We both nodded. 'I spoke to Ian earlier. Think they're planning on taking him out some-where this afternoon. You know –' she gestured towards the garden. 'With their dog.'

'Good idea,' I said. 'I'll just gather his last bits, then shall I? Love –' I turned to Mike. 'You want to call the kids inside?'

But for all my resolve, it was clear that we would be derailed anyway, as became obvious as soon as we all trooped to the waiting car. There was no answer to it – no opportunity to make it any less painful. Olivia was going to have to say goodbye to her brother. And as soon as she realised – she'd known for some time, but it was horribly real now – she became instantly, dramatically, genuinely inconsolable.

'Please don't go, Ash!' she sobbed as he solemnly bent to hug her. 'You don't have to! Please don't make him, Casey! Please don't!'

'I gotta go, Livs,' he said, his voice gruff with emotion, as Anna – thank God for Anna at that moment – calmly took him by the hand, and led him to the waiting car, while I prised Olivia from him and hugged her tight to me.

Ashton climbed into the back seat of the car, and Anna helped him with his seat belt, and as she did so, I had to stop myself from fussing about the journey, and wanting to dash in and get him a travel-sickness pill. He'd be fine. It wasn't far. He'd never *actually* been car sick. And then I watched as Mike stopped to say goodbye through the open window, the cacophony of Olivia's wails almost drowning him out. I got the gist though: 'Don't be scared, mate. You're a great kid … they're going to love you … just like we do. We all do. Keep in touch …'

Then it was my turn, once Mike had taken Olivia from me, and once again, I had to speak to myself very, very sternly. 'Hey, love,' I said. 'I am *so* going to miss you, you know that?'

He nodded glumly, his face contorted with the effort of not crying, as he wound his arms around my neck to say goodbye. And as I kissed him he did something entirely unexpected. He put his lips to my ear and whispered, 'I love you'.

'Right,' said Anna. 'Time to go, I think.' She started the engine. 'I'll phone you,' I told him, almost too choked to speak now. 'In a few days, when you're settled in, okay? Love you too, Ash. So much. Take care of yourself, okay?'

The car purred from the kerb, prompting fresh sobs from Olivia. 'I love you, Ash! I love you!' she screamed as the car moved, and as he turned to mouth it back, I could see his own tears begin to flow.

I took Olivia from Mike and set her down on the pavement, then knelt down and hugged her and cried my eyes out.

* * *

I barely slept a wink that night, which would have been no surprise to anyone. How could I, knowing we had to do it all again with Olivia in the morning? If it had been hard with Ashton, I knew it would be even worse with his little sister. For all that I would worry about Ash, I was comforted by the knowledge that there was a strength in him, a sense of self, that I knew would see him through. But little Olivia – *tiny* Olivia – with all her funny little mannerisms; she was so young and so vulnerable and so much the baby, that I couldn't help but fret about how she would fare. Didn't matter how much faith I had in Mick and Sandie. Saying goodbye to her was going to be so hard.

It wasn't made easier by the fact that, perhaps as expected, she'd been so overcome by Ash's leaving.

'Did they tooken him somewhere else because he's bin naughty?' she asked Mike, almost as soon as we'd got back inside the house.

'Not at all,' he reassured her. 'Quite the opposite, in fact. He's gone to Kerry and Ian so they can take care of him,' he explained. 'Don't you remember? Like Anna said? So they can make things nice for him again?'

'But why couldn't Ash come with *me*?' she persisted.

'Was it that bad mens? Did the bad mens say he couldn't, cos he bummed me?'

Inspiration came from somewhere. 'Not at all,' I said firmly. 'He's gone with Ian and Kerry, because their own little boy has gone away now. So they're very lonely, and Anna knew that lovely Ash would cheer them up.'

It was pathetic. It was all wrong, and perhaps I shouldn't have said it. But, even so, it really seemed to help.

Mike, up before me on the Sunday morning, was already one step ahead of me. The first car that pulled up wasn't Anna's, but Lauren's father's. Dropping Kieron and Lauren off, as Mike had asked, bless him, to provide me with some much-needed moral support. Summoned likewise, Riley and Levi showed up on the doorstep moments later, so it was in the middle of a very crowded and noisy kitchen that Olivia, somewhat sleepy, after the trauma of yesterday, shyly handed me an envelope.

'It's for you an' Mike,' she said. 'An' you're not allowed to open it till after. It's a secret,' she added, smiling bravely. I gathered her up onto my hip and then scrutinised the envelope. 'This is beautiful,' I said. 'Goodness me, you've worked hard.'

It was too. She had covered it with carefully coloured pictures. 'These is butterflies, an' these are flowers and that was sposed to be a bird there but it don' look much like one, because I got into a kerfluffle with the wings.'

'It's beautiful,' I said. 'Look, Riley, isn't it beautiful?'

Riley nodded. 'You are so good at drawing,' she told Olivia. 'Keep it up, okay? One day you might be a great artist and –'

'Helloooo!' came a voice then, through the still-open front door.

It was Anna. Olivia immediately began whimpering. 'Don't wanna go, Casey!' she mumbled, burying her face in my neck.

'Come on, sweetheart,' I said, trooping after Mike into the hallway, to find Anna standing on the doorstep, holding a large cardboard box.

'Well, hello,' said Mike, obviously seeing something in her expression. 'What have you got in there, then, Anna?'

'A surprise,' Anna answered. I felt Olivia lift her head. 'For a certain little girl,' Anna added. 'From Mick and Sandie. Hey, Olivia, do you want to take a look?'

Anna leaned down and carefully placed the box on the floor, while I let Olivia down again.

'Here,' said Anna. 'Open up this flap here, like this. It's a very important present for an important little girl. You see, you're not the only one moving to Mick and Sandie's today …'

Olivia pulled open the first flap, then the other, to reveal, in the corner, sitting trembling on a square of blanket, a tiny brown and white terrier puppy.

'Ooh, a doggy!' Olivia squealed in delight.

'A very *little* doggy,' explained Anna, 'who needs a special little girl to take very good care of him. Think you can do that?'

'Ohh!' Olivia squealed again, as Levi toddled up to join her. 'Oh, he's so sweet! What's his name?'

'He hasn't got one yet,' Anna told her. 'Mick and Sandie said that would be your job. So you'll have to start thinking right away.'

A stroke of genius, I decided, as we began gathering possessions and loading them into the back of Anna's car. Because suddenly the atmosphere, previously so sad, had changed completely. Far from crying now, Olivia was practically skipping to the roadside, and leapt into the car without so much as a backwards glance. All her attention was focussed on the cardboard box beside her. Even Polly, at her side for almost every waking hour, had been relegated – dumped unceremoniously on the other rear seat. 'You sit over there, Poll,' she ordered. 'So's the doggie can sit by me. All right, liccle doggie?' she crooned. 'You okay?'

It seemed almost an afterthought to say goodbyes to us. 'Bye Mike! Bye Casey! Bye ev-ryone elses!' she sang. 'I'll tell you doggie's name when I've thinked it!'

And after kissing us all in turn and promising to send us pictures, she was off down the road, waving happily.

I was so astounded, I just stood and stared after her for some moments, unable to fully comprehend what had just happened.

'Oh, Mum,' said Riley, laughing, ever the wag at such junctures. 'You should see your face! It's an absolute picture!' I blinked at her. 'Really,' she went on. 'It is – it's priceless! You really were expecting a full-on drama, weren't you?'

Seeing my daughter laughing at me brought me to my senses. 'Well!' I grumbled huffily, as both she and Kieron continued laughing. 'Wouldn't *you*?' I noticed Mike was laughing too, then, so I huffed a bit more. 'I mean, fancy being upstaged by a bloody puppy!'

* * *

'That's attachment disorder for you,' John Fulshaw coun-
selled wisely, on the Monday. I'd called him for a debrief. I
didn't really need to, not yet, but the house was much too
quiet, and, as much as anything, I was glad to hear his voice.
'That's the thing,' he went on. 'You invest so much in these
kids, and you worry so much about how they'll miss you,
don't you? And there's no doubt,' he added diplomatically,
'that they will. But they'll be fine. You know that, don't
you? You've done wonders with them, both of you.'

'*Some* good, at least, I hope,' I said. 'At least our best.
Which is all we *can* do ...'

'Hey, but listen, Casey. Actually, I'm very glad you
called.'

I felt my hand grip the phone just a little tighter as he
said that. *Uh oh*, I thought, *what's gone wrong?* 'Go on,' I
said warily, crossing my fingers. 'What is it?'

'Well, actually,' he said, 'it's something quite strange.'
His tone was bright, though. I mentally relaxed. Just a
little. 'In fact, I've never come across something like this
before.'

'Like what?'

'Well apparently, this eight-year-old boy has just turned
up at social services – he made his own way there, by all
accounts – and demanded that he be taken into care.'

'And?' I said, waiting for the punch-line.

It came.

'Well, what do *you* think, Casey?' he said, laughing.

Epilogue

'Dear Casey, I luv you soooooooo much and so does Ash. We luv your cudduls and your kisses but when Myk kist us his chin ticculs. We will miss you and fink about you all the tym, keep ar picturs on the wall, lots of love from Olivia Wardhill age 7

xxxxxxxxxxxxxxxxxxxx'

This letter takes pride of place underneath the photograph of Olivia and Ashton that we took on the beach in South Wales. It still makes me smile every time I walk by it, as I remember their squeals and their anxious little faces when experiencing 'the seaside' for the very first time.

Two years down the line, both children are doing exceptionally well, and to my great relief, my fears about their separation have been laid to rest. Their respective carers have proved to be sensitive and full of wisdom about the children's needs, and though they live apart, they are still very much in touch with each other and, as I write, their bond still remains strong. We see them too; they still come to visit us in the school holidays and I can't help but feel so, so proud of them.

As for the disclosures made by the children when they were with us, Olivia, during her subsequent time with a counsellor, was actually very revealing. As I write, there have still been no arrests, it's true, but even though officially it's no longer of concern to us, John tells me that social services are still amassing evidence and that it's 'only a matter of time now'. So I'm still very confident that the biggest villain in all this will, one day, have that day in court.

I knew I would miss the children dreadfully – when they left, the house suddenly felt so quiet! – but having a second grandson to fuss over, not to mention our gorgeous Levi, helped keep me busy when I needed to be most. And all too soon, of course, came along the next 'unfosterable' foster child. One thing's for sure about my chosen career – the work never, ever dries up …

It also helped to feel that, in giving Ashton and Olivia a loving home, we'd played a part in something so important. Had these children not been rescued from their hellish lives when they were, there's little doubt that, as would also have been true for their younger siblings, they would have continued to be abused, and perhaps scarred to such a point that they would never live normal adult lives. As it turned out, they not only found their own way to a brighter future, they also ensured that the next generation would not become little prisoners themselves.

TOPICS FOR READING-GROUP DISCUSSION

1. Some doctors claim that ADHD does not exist and that other diagnoses are often ignored because of the knee-jerk tendency to cover all bases with the label. How do you feel about this? Should such a condition be treated with powerful medication, or should parents and teachers take more responsibility to work on behaviour?

2. At what age should it be spelled out to a child that they are going into care? Should a social worker always be truthful about the reasons for a child's removal from their home? Are there any circumstances when the truth should be hidden?

3. Mike and I were deeply shocked that children as abused and neglected as Ashton and Olivia could have existed 'under the radar' for so long. Do you think modern society contributes to that? Are communities weaker than they once were?

4. Our grown-up son Kieron was deeply traumatised by some of Ashton's and Olivia's behaviours, so much so that he moved out. Although he said he was planning to do so anyway, to move in with his girlfriend, I felt guilty and upset. How do you feel about the impact that fostering has on a carer's own children? How do you think you would feel in that situation?

5. At the end of *Little Prisoners*, siblings Ashton and Olivia have to be placed in separate long-term families to give them both the best chance of leading happier lives, even though it means they will lose each other. How does that make you feel? Do you agree with the decision?

CASEY WATSON

One woman determined to
make a difference.

Read Casey's poignant
memoirs and be inspired.

Five-year-old Justin was desperate and helpless

Six years after being taken into care, Justin has had 20 failed placements. Casey and her family are his last hope.

THE BOY NO ONE LOVED

A damaged girl haunted by her past

Sophia pushes Casey to the limits, threatening the safety of the whole family. Can Casey make a difference in time?

CRYING FOR HELP

Abused siblings who do not know what it means to be loved

With new-found security and trust, Casey helps Ashton and Olivia to rebuild their lives.

LITTLE PRISONERS

Branded 'vicious and evil', eight-year-old Spencer asks to be taken into care

Casey and her family are disgusted: kids aren't born evil. Despite the challenges Spencer brings, they are determined to help him find a loving home.

TOO HURT TO STAY

A young girl secretly caring for her mother

Abigail has been dealing with pressures no child should face. Casey has the difficult challenge of helping her to learn to let go.

A heartrending story of a child secretly caring for her severely disabled mother

Mummy's Little Helper

CASEY WATSON

SUNDAY TIMES BESTSELLING AUTHOR

MUMMY'S LITTLE HELPER

SUNDAY TIMES BESTSELLING AUTHOR

CASEY WATSON

Breaking the Silence

Two little boys, lost and unloved. One woman determined to make a difference

Two boys with an unlikely bond

With Georgie and Jenson, Casey is facing her toughest test yet.

BREAKING THE SILENCE

A teenage mother and baby in need of a loving home

At fourteen, Emma is just a child herself – and one who's never been properly mothered.

A LAST KISS FOR MUMMY

Eleven-year-old Tyler has stabbed his stepmother and has nowhere to go.

With his birth mother dead and a father who doesn't want him, what can be done to stop his young life spiralling out of control?

NOWHERE TO GO

What is the secret behind Imogen's silence?

Discover the shocking and devastating past of a child with severe behavioural problems.

THE GIRL WITHOUT A VOICE

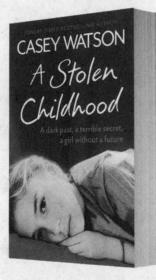

Kiara appears tired and distressed, and the school wants Casey to take her under her wing for a while.

On the surface, everything points to a child who is upset that her parents have separated. The horrific truth, however, shocks Casey to the core.

· A STOLEN CHILDHOOD

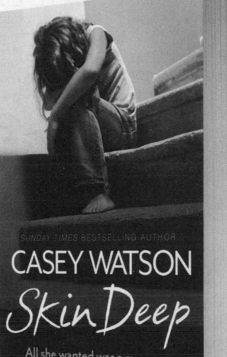

SUNDAY TIMES BESTSELLING AUTHOR

CASEY WATSON

Skin Deep

All she wanted was a mummy,
but was she too ugly to be loved?

Eight-year-old Flip, who is being raised by
her single, alcoholic mother, comes to Casey
after a fire at their home.

Flip has Foetal Alcohol Syndrome (FAS), which
Casey has come across before, but it soon turns out
that this is just the tip of the iceberg . . .

SKIN DEEP

AVAILABLE AS E-BOOK ONLY

Cameron is a sweet boy with a great sense of humour; he seems happy in his skin – making him rather different from most of the other children Casey has cared for.

But what happens when Cameron disappears? Will Casey's worst fears be realised?

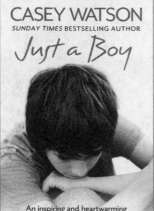

JUST A BOY

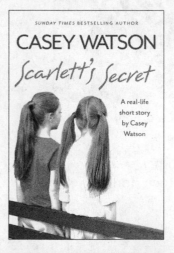

Jade and Scarlett, seventeen-year-old twins, share a terrible secret.

Can Casey help them to come to terms with the truth and rediscover their sibling connection?

SCARLETT'S SECRET

AVAILABLE AS E-BOOK ONLY

Nathan has a sometime alter ego called Jenny who is the only one who knows the secrets of his disturbed past.

But where is Jenny when she is most needed?

NO PLACE FOR NATHAN

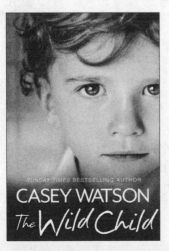

Angry and hurting, eight-year-old Connor is from a broken home

As streetwise as they come, he's determined to cause trouble. But Casey is convinced there is a frightened child beneath the swagger.

THE WILD CHILD

FEEL HEART.
FEEL HOPE.
READ CASEY.

Discover more about Casey Watson.
Visit www.caseywatson.co.uk

Find Casey Watson on **f** & **t**

Moving Memoirs

Stories of hope, courage and the power of love...

If you loved this book, then you will love our
Moving Memoirs eNewsletter

Sign up to...

- Be the first to hear about new books

- Get sneak previews from your favourite authors

- Read exclusive interviews

- Be entered into our monthly prize draw to win one
  of our latest releases before it's even hit the shops!

Sign up at

www.moving-memoirs.com